HAMLYN
COOKERY SCHOOL

HAMLYN
COOKERY SCHOOL

150 great step-by-step recipes

hamlyn

An Hachette Livre UK Company

First published in Great Britain in 2007 by Hamlyn,
a division of Octopus Publishing Group Ltd
2–4 Heron Quays, London E14 4JP

Recipes written by Joanna Farrow, with contributions from
Sara Lewis and David Morgan.

ISBN-13: 978-0-600-61651-1
ISBN-10: 0-600-61651-7

A CIP catalogue record for this book is available
from the British Library.

Printed and bound in China

10 9 8 7 6 5 4 3 2 1

NOTES

Both metric and imperial measurements have been given
in all recipes. Use one set of measurements only, and not a
mixture of both.

Standard level spoon measurements are used in all recipes.

1 tablespoon = one 15 ml spoon
1 teaspoon = one 5 ml spoon

The Department of Health advises that eggs should not be
consumed raw. This book contains dishes made with raw or
lightly cooked eggs. It is prudent for vulnerable people such
as pregnant and nursing mothers, invalids, the elderly,
babies and young children to avoid uncooked or lightly
cooked dishes made with eggs. Once prepared, these
dishes should be kept refrigerated and used promptly.

This book includes dishes made with nuts and nut
derivatives. It is advisable for customers with known
allergic reactions to nuts and nut derivatives and those
who may be potentially vulnerable to these allergies, such
as pregnant and nursing mothers, invalids, the elderly,
babies and children, to avoid dishes made with nuts and
nut oils. It is also prudent to check the labels of pre-
prepared ingredients for the possible inclusion of nut
derivatives.

Ovens should be preheated to the specified temperature; if
you are using a fan-assisted oven follow the manufacturer's
instructions for adjusting the time and the temperature.

Contents

Introduction

You may find the idea of cooking a recipe from scratch rather daunting. But, as with any other skill, it is perfectly possible to learn. True, it takes patience, practice and the odd failure, but soon you will be preparing meals with flair.

Easy does it

Cooking can and should be a relaxing pastime. If you have little or no experience in the kitchen beyond boiling the kettle or flipping down the toaster you might not agree. However, there really is no better way to unwind after a busy or stressful day than to pour yourself a glass of wine and prepare dinner. It doesn't matter whether it's a basic pasta dish or a ten-step gourmet recipe – the effect is the same. The simple actions of chopping, stirring, following a recipe and creating something delicious should be sufficient to make your stress levels drop. You can then sit down with a sense of satisfaction as you tuck into a delicious, fresh, homemade meal that will knock the socks off anything you take out of the freezer and watch spinning around the microwave for five minutes.

Kitchen confidence

If your kitchen is the least visited room in the house, you might want to become a little better acquainted with it before you start 'cookery school'. When you are following a recipe, you need to know exactly where everything is kept and what equipment you have in your cupboards. For example, you might decide to try some baking, but it might not be such an easy or enjoyable experience if you don't have a food processor. The key is to think about what you will actually be cooking and what you might need to have to hand to achieve it. There are hundreds of different kitchen gadgets on the market, but there's no point giving valuable kitchen space to an ice cream maker or fondue set if you are never going to use them. Choose practical equipment that will be used regularly and then make sure that

everything is easily accessible. It is also important not to wait until the afternoon of the dinner party or special meal to find out how everything works: always have a trial run beforehand. Here are a few more tips to help things go smoothly:

- Keep your cupboards well stocked with essentials and make a note of things as they are about to run out so that you can stock up next time you shop.
- Always check the recipe before you begin cooking to make sure you have all the ingredients.
- Prepare all the ingredients for a recipe before you begin – weighing, chopping, slicing and so on.
- Get to know your oven because every one has its own little quirks, and temperatures, and therefore cooking times, can vary between models. Remember, too, that there's a big difference between regular and fan ovens so you will need to adjust your cooking times accordingly.
- If anything needs to be defrosted, do this in plenty of time by transferring it to the refrigerator.

Cooking by the book

If you love the idea of being able to prepare meals but just don't have the confidence to do it, this is the perfect book for you. It will guide you through every stage of becoming a competent cook, beginning with all the basics so you can be well prepared for your first serious foray into the kitchen. This includes descriptions of all the basic equipment and ingredients you might need.

It's a good idea to arm yourself with some basic information before you attempt anything too ambitious. Learning to cook is a gradual process and you build on your expertise and knowledge with each new recipe, so there's absolutely no point in challenging yourself with a steak and kidney pie before you've mastered the art of pastry making. Start with straightforward recipes and simple techniques and you will find that you quickly build up to more complicated dishes.

The first section of the book is dedicated to the basics. You will be guided through all the information you will need to help you on your way to becoming an accomplished cook. You will begin by learning how

to make stocks and basic sauces, which are absolutely essential to so many different recipes in every type of cuisine. From casseroles and soups to pasta, there's no underestimating the importance of a good stock or sauce. You will also learn how to choose the best cuts of meat and the freshest fish, and then how to prepare and serve them. Finally, the basics of cake and pastry making are introduced to complete your cookery course. The following chapters of the book will then take you through a different type of food or dish, with a wide selection of recipes that incorporate some of the techniques learned earlier.

Mission accomplished

If the idea of cooking Shellfish Laksa (see page 102) or Thai Chicken Curry (see page 191) would normally make you feel faint, fear not. You will soon be attempting dishes such as these with a new level of culinary confidence. Having mastered the basic skills, you will able to tackle more complicated techniques and will slowly build up your repertoire. If, each time you attempt a recipe for the first time, you think of it as a combination of enjoyment and a challenge you won't go far wrong. Empty plates and nods of approval at the end of a meal will make all the effort seem worthwhile. And remember: the cook never does the washing up!

THE BASICS

Equipment

To cook successfully you need to invest in a basic range of good-quality tools and utensils. This need not be extensive – a few well-chosen items are not only essential for best results but will also save unnecessary time and effort.

Baking tins

Some baking tins have bright, shiny surfaces that deflect the heat from the contents so they do not scorch, whereas others have dark finishes that absorb and hold the heat. Tin plate is widely used for bakeware. Aluminium, a good conductor of heat, is more expensive than tin. Nonstick surfaces, applied to either tin or aluminium, are hardwearing but can easily be damaged by metal implements. Choose tins, including cake tins (see page 50), that are sturdy, are smooth inside with no crevices and that have rolled edges to make them easier and safer to handle.

Flan tins

For quiches, pies and tarts. Flan tins are preferable to porcelain flan dishes, because they conduct heat effectively, which prevents soggy pastry.

Patty tins

A patty tin is a sheet of cup-shaped hollows for baking tartlets and small cakes.

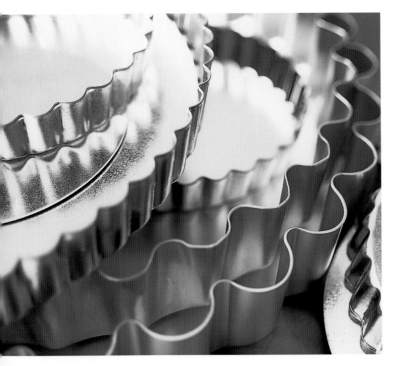

Pie dishes

A classic pie dish for cooking sweet and savoury pies is oval-shaped with sloping sides and a wide, flat rim for holding the pastry lid. It should have a capacity of 1.2 litres (2 pints). A pie plate is shallower and round.

Blenders and food processors

A food processor or blender removes a lot of the effort involved in chopping vegetables, mixing pastes, pastry making and puréeing cooked ingredients. It reduces the amount of time you have to handle pastry dough, which can be helpful in hot weather or if you have warm hands. Take care not to over mix the fat with the flour, however. A few short bursts will allow you to judge the breadcrumb stage. You may find you need more water than if you are mixing by hand – add any water little by little rather than all at once.

A small food processor, or a larger one with a small inner bowl, is ideal for spice blends and chopping small quantities of herbs and nuts. A hand-held electric immersion blender is great for blending and puréeing a sauce or soup while it is still in the saucepan.

Chopping boards

Have two chopping boards, one made from hard wood, such as maple, for most tasks, and the other for the preparation of raw meat. This board should be made from white, non-porous material that can be cleaned with hot water and a little bleach. Always wash boards and knives between handling raw and cooked food.

Choose a wooden board at least 4 cm (1½ inches) thick. Ideally, the grain should run in the opposite direction to that on the reinforced ends. Melamine boards look attractive but their hard surfaces soon blunt blades and may cause knives to slip.

Clingfilm

Useful for wrapping food to be refrigerated, clingfilm is essential for wrapping pastry while it 'rests'. It's important to allow pastry to rest before it is cooked so it does not shrink and become distorted. If the surface of the pastry comes into contact with the air it will form a skin, which will crack when rolled out.

Colander

Choose a stainless steel colander with a long handle and stable base so that it can be held firmly while you drain pasta or vegetables. A colander can also be used to steam food if you do not have a steamer.

Fish slice

Indispensable for lifting and turning all kinds of food, including bacon rashers, fried eggs, pieces of meat and, of course, fillets of fish.

Garlic press

This useful tool finely crushes garlic cloves by forcing the flesh through a series of tiny holes, thereby releasing the full flavour. It also saves your hands from coming into contact with the garlic juices and avoids their pungent aroma lingering on the skin.

Grater

Multi-purpose graters come in box shapes or as single flat sheets. They have different perforations for preparing various kinds of ingredients. The fine holes are used for grating whole spices, chocolate, Parmesan and citrus rind, and the medium to large holes for grating fresh root ginger, other cheeses and vegetables. Mini graters may be used for whole nutmegs, but ordinary graters will work just as well.

Knives

A good set of knives is essential. It is worth getting a well-made set of stainless steel or carbon steel knives, forged in one piece with a riveted wooden or plastic handle. To avoid dulling the blades, they should be sharpened regularly and kept separately in a wooden block or on a magnetic rack.

Bread knife

This knife with a serrated edge is useful for slicing bread and cakes because it does not tear the food.

Chopping knife

A heavy, wide-bladed knife is ideal for chopping vegetables, herbs and other ingredients. It is also

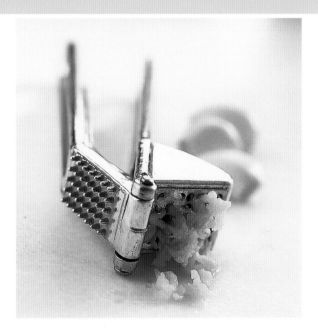

useful for transferring chopped ingredients from the chopping board to the cooking pan. The side of the blade can be used for crushing garlic.

General kitchen knife and paring knife

A medium-sized, all-purpose knife, usually 15–25 cm (6–10 inches) long, can be used for chopping, slicing and cutting all kinds of ingredients. A small paring knife is ideal for preparing fruit and vegetables.

Masher

You need this useful tool for mashing potatoes and other root vegetables, such as swedes and parsnips.

Measuring jug

This is a standardized measure with a pouring lip, usually marked in both metric and imperial quantities. Choose a jug made from heatproof glass that can withstand boiling liquids and so you can see clearly how much is in the jug.

Measuring spoons

Ingredients are often given in teaspoons or tablespoons. All spoon measures in the recipes in this book are assumed to be level (1 teaspoon equals 5 ml and 1 tablespoon equals 15 ml). Buy yourself a set of measuring spoons so you can accurately add ¼ or ½ teaspoon quantities as necessary, as well as larger quantities of both liquid and dry ingredients.

Mixing bowls

Always use a bowl that is large enough to hold comfortably all the ingredients you will be using and that is heavy enough to sit firmly on the work surface without slipping away from you when stirring or beating. Heatproof glass or ceramic bowls are most useful. Keep a couple of small bowls for beating eggs or holding small quantities of food. A small heatproof glass bowl, which will fit snugly over a saucepan, is ideal for melting chocolate.

Palette knife

Consisting of a long, flexible, round-ended metal blade set in a handle, a palette knife is essential for achieving smooth, even coverage – for example, when coating a cake with icing or ganache. It is also useful for scraping mixtures from bowls and flipping over pancakes. You'll need both large and small knives.

Paper piping bags

Perfect for piping decorations directly on to food, paper piping bags are easy to make. Cut a 25 cm (10 inch) square of greaseproof paper or nonstick baking paper and fold it diagonally in half to make a triangle. Cut along the folded line. Holding the centre of the long edge towards you, curl the right-hand point of the triangle over to meet the centre point, forming a cone. Bring the left-hand point over the cone so the three points meet. Fold the paper over several times at the points to stop it unravelling. Half-fill the bag with melted chocolate or icing and fold down the open end to secure before snipping off the tip of the bag. Test the flow and snip off a little more for a thicker flow.

Pasta server

A long-handled, stainless steel spoon is designed to transfer pasta or noodles from saucepan to serving dish. It has teeth that grasp the pasta and a hole that allows the cooking liquid to drain back into the pan.

Pastry brushes

You will need a fairly broad brush to apply melted butter to sheets of pastry and a finer brush for more detailed work, such as applying glazes to decorations.

Pestle and mortar

This is used for grinding herbs and whole spices and can be made of marble, which does not absorb flavours, wood or ceramic.

Pots and pans

A set of three or four saucepans is all you need. Always use a heavy-based saucepan for sauce making and, indeed, for most other types of cooking because it will conduct heat more efficiently. Some pans have a capacity gauge inside, which is useful if you're reducing a stock or sauce by a certain amount.

A large pan – 5–6 litres (8½–10 pints) – is suitable for making stocks. Medium pans – about 2 litres (3½ pints) – are suitable for most sauces and can also serve as a bain marie with a heatproof bowl resting over it.

All pans come in a choice of materials. Copper is perfect for sauce making as it conducts heat so well. Stainless steel is the most popular as it is lightweight and easy to clean. The best stainless steel pans have a

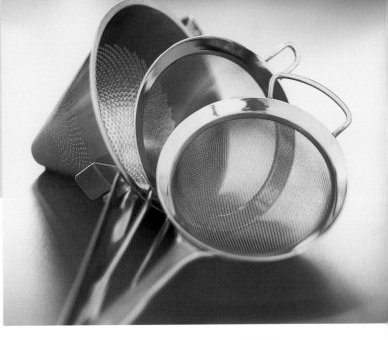

steel-enclosed aluminium base for good heat conduction. Aluminium should not be used for cooking fruit and acidic ingredients, which react with the metal.

Frying pan
Ideal for browning, choose a pan made of heavy gauge, heat-conducting metal. It should have a wide, flat base, shallow sides and a long handle.

Stove-top grill pan
Dry-frying with a cast-iron grill pan is a fast and simple way to cook. The pan is preheated and seasoned food is cooked directly on the ridged or flat surface. Food can be cooked without the addition of any fat and may be marinated first for extra flavour.

Rolling pin
Essential for rolling out pastry, pasta and bread dough, rolling pins can be made of wood, plastic or marble.

Scales
Getting the right proportion of ingredients is actually more important than the precise quantities.

Sieves and strainers
A fine-mesh stainless steel or nylon sieve is essential for sifting and straining. It can also be used for puréeing, by rubbing cooked ingredients through the mesh with the back of a ladle or wooden spoon. Use a metal sieve to sift flour and other ingredients into a mixing bowl. A sieve is also useful for dusting finished desserts with icing sugar.

Conical strainers are good for sauce making as the liquid strains through the base rather than splashing all over the work surface. Choose one with small holes for straining stocks, while a wire mesh sieve is good for extracting juices from fruit or vegetable pulps and gives a velvety-smooth consistency.

Spoons and whisks
A slotted metal spoon is good for draining ingredients after frying or for skimming fat or froth from the surface of a stock.

Some cooks prefer to use a balloon or coiled whisk for thickening sauces. In general, however, a wooden spoon is invaluable for beating, mixing and stirring. Choose one made of close-grained wood with a thin edge that allows you to get to the bottom of the pan.

Balloon whisks are good for blending ingredients, whisking egg whites and incorporating air into batter mixtures. Keep an assortment of different sizes but avoid very large ones, which are less effective. If you are a keen cake-maker, invest in an electric whisk.

Steamer
This useful item consists of a perforated container that holds food to be steamed, placed inside a pan containing a small amount of boiling water. Make sure it has a tight-fitting lid.

Tongs and a two-pronged fork
Perfect for picking up items of hot food or for turning food when you are grilling or barbecuing. A metal fork with long prongs will hold meat or poultry firmly while it is lifted to or from a roasting pan or casserole.

Vegetable peeler
In addition to removing the skin from vegetables and fruit, a vegetable peeler can also be used to pare carrot or courgette ribbons or to make chocolate curls or Parmesan shavings.

Wok
These large, round-bottomed pans are used in oriental cooking, especially stir-frying. They can be nonstick or steel. Choose one about 35 cm (14 inches) across.

Wooden spatula
This has a wide, blunt blade and is useful for moving ingredients around in a pan or bowl.

Essential ingredients

A few key ingredients form the basis of most recipes, so here is a guide to the ones you should always aim to keep in your store cupboard or refrigerator. Buy the best you can – quality will affect flavour.

Butter

Always use unsalted butter for sauces and cakes, although lightly salted butter may act as a substitute if you run out. Unsalted butter imparts a good flavour and is free from the additives contained in many other adulterated spreads and margarines. Salted butter has a less creamy flavour and is more likely to burn; it will also affect the flavour, especially in cake making. Margarines and non-dairy spreads may be used, if necessary, but check they are suitable for baking before you buy.

Cream

Often used to add a velvety-smooth finish to a sauce. Provided it's really fresh, neither double nor single cream should separate, even when boiled, unless it's mixed with a high proportion of acidic ingredients. Crème fraîche, which makes a good alternative when a tangier, but still creamy flavour is required, is best not cooked at high temperatures.

Eggs

Whenever possible, use really fresh, preferably free-range, organic eggs. This is particularly important in a recipe such as Crème Anglaise (see page 227) where the eggs provide colour and flavour. Always use eggs at room temperature because they will give more volume and are less likely to curdle in creamed mixtures.

Flour

For most recipes, plain white flour is best. Self-raising flour provides a softer, sponge-like texture and should be used for suet crust. It is also the kind most widely used in cake making – some self-raising flours are sold specially for cake making. Wholemeal flour, or a mixture of half wholemeal and half white, can be used for shortcrust pastry, but it tends to give a heavy, crumbly dough, which can be difficult to handle. Puff, flaky or rough puff pastries are usually made with strong plain flour because the high levels of gluten give the dough more elasticity and strength.

Herbs

Fresh herbs have far better flavour than dried ones but
are best used as soon as possible after buying or
picking. Delicate herbs deteriorate after several days
in the refrigerator.

Oils

You don't need a huge supply of oils in the cupboard.
Richly flavoured extra virgin olive oil is ideal for many
Mediterranean-style sauces, while a light olive oil is
more suitable for a sauce in which you need a good oil
but don't want its flavour to dominate – in mayonnaise,
for example. Choose mildly flavoured oil, such as
sunflower or groundnut oil, for other recipes, including
Indian and Asian-style sauces. A little sesame oil adds
a delicious flavour to Asian dishes, although it cannot
be used for frying because of its low smoking point.
Nut oils, such as walnut and hazelnut, are particularly
good in recipes where you want to emphasize a nutty
flavour – buy them as and when required.

Stock

For the best flavour use homemade stock. Don't be put
off by this: stocks are inexpensive and easy to make,
and it's not difficult to get into the habit of making
them. Use leftover bones from a roast or ask your
butcher for bones when you're in the shop, and use a
selection of fresh vegetables from the market. If you
don't need the stock for a few days, freeze for a ready
supply. Cartons or tubs of ready-made stock are a good
alternative but tend to be expensive for the amount you
get. Concentrated liquid stock is a good standby, as are
good-quality cubes and powders. These are often quite
salty, though, and should therefore be used sparingly.

Sugar

Well-flavoured sugars, such as light and dark
muscovado and molasses sugar, impart plenty of extra
flavour to cakes and combine well with chocolate,
spices and treacle. Occasionally, muscovado sugar
hardens during storage. So that you can cook with it,
pop the pack in the microwave and give it short bursts
on medium power until it softens.

Successful sauces

A good sauce will transform the most simple dish into a lively and interesting meal. A well-made sauce complements and enhances the food, adding flavour, colour, texture and moisture without overpowering or detracting from it.

Thickening sauces

There is a number of ways in which a sauce can be thickened. Sometimes it is achieved in the first step of a recipe, as in a roux, but sometimes it is a finishing step, using ingredients such as egg yolks, cream and butter. The most important rule for a successful sauce is to avoid over-thickening. A sauce made cloyingly thick with flour or cornflour is unpalatable and can ruin a whole dish. As a guide, most sauces are sufficiently thickened when they thinly coat the back of a wooden spoon. Let the sauce cool slightly on the spoon then run your finger along it – it should leave a clear impression.

Roux

A blend of butter and flour, lightly cooked together before the liquid is added, as in a Béchamel Sauce (see page 20). If the roux is cooked a little more it forms the base of a velouté sauce, as in Tarragon Cream Sauce (see page 163). If it is cooked further still, it is used for brown sauces.

Beurre manié

This is also a mixture of butter and flour, but here they are kneaded together in a bowl to make a paste and then whisked into the cooked sauce until it thickens. It is a useful method for thickening a disappointingly thin sauce or a stew or casserole in which the juice is very thin. Use about 15 g (½ oz) each of softened butter and plain flour to 600 ml (1 pint) of liquid.

Butter

Whisking a little chilled butter into a finished sauce thickens it slightly and gives it a lighter flavour and glossier finish.

Cornflour

Cornflour must be blended with a little water, stock or juice before it is added to a sauce. It's rarely used in traditional sauces but sometimes crops up in Asian-style ones.

Egg yolks and cream

These are good for adding extra flavour and richness to a thin sauce, particularly those with a stock base. Blend 2 egg yolks with 150 ml (¼ pint) of single cream and add a ladleful of hot but not boiling sauce. Tip the mixture into the pan and cook over a gentle heat, whisking or stirring until it is slightly thickened.

Reducing

As long as it doesn't include eggs or yogurt or any ingredients that are likely to curdle, a thin stock or sauce can be reduced and thickened by rapid boiling. If

you are reducing a stock, don't start boiling it until you have removed the bones and so on. The reducing time will vary depending on the amount of liquid, so keep an eye on the pan. If necessary, skim off any froth on the surface using a slotted spoon and don't season the sauce until you have reduced it as this often intensifies the flavours.

Puréeing
Some sauces, particularly those made from fruit or vegetables, can be thickened by blending the ingredients, either in a food processor or blender, or using an immersion blender.

Bouquet garni
Tying a mixture of herbs in a bouquet garni means you can easily remove it from the sauce after cooking. A classic bouquet garni includes bay leaves, sprigs of thyme and parsley stalks, which are wrapped in a length of celery or leek and tied with string.

Skinning tomatoes
The best way to skin tomatoes is to put them in a bowl and cover them with boiling water. Leave them for 1–2 minutes or until the skins split, then spear one tomato with a sharp knife to check that the skin peels away easily before draining them all.

Simple stocks and sauces
Any sauce tastes better if you use a homemade stock. Don't be put off by this. Stocks are easy and cheap to make, and it's not hard to get into the habit of making them. Use leftover bones from a roast or ask your butcher for bones when you're in the shop, or use a selection of fresh vegetables when they pile up in the refrigerator. If you don't need the stock for a few days, freeze it for a ready supply. Cartons or tubs of ready-made stock make a good alternative but are expensive for the amount you get. Concentrated liquid stocks are an adequate standby, as are good-quality cubes and powders. These are often salty, though, and should therefore be used sparingly.

A selection of good basic stocks and sauces that every cook should have in their repertoire follows. Some sauces accompany certain foods naturally – parsley sauce complements fish perfectly, for example – and you will find these sauces in the relevant chapters of the book.

Basic stock recipes

A good, homemade stock is the foundation for a truly tasty and healthy meal. Whether you're adding it to a casserole, making soup or gravy, the flavour will be far superior to anything derived from a stock cube.

Beef stock

When you buy a piece of beef, get the bones as well and ask the butcher to cut them into manageable pieces. Cheap cuts of beef and trimmings can be used instead of bones, but this tends to be more expensive. For a dark, richly coloured stock, roast the bones in a preheated oven, 200°C (400°F), Gas Mark 6, for 45 minutes beforehand.

Preparation time 10 minutes
Cooking time 3 hours
Makes about 1 litre (1¾ pints)

750 g (1½ lb) beef bones
1 large onion, unpeeled and quartered
1 large carrot, roughly chopped
2 celery sticks, roughly chopped
1 bouquet garni
1 teaspoon black peppercorns

❶ Put the bones into a large, heavy-based saucepan with the onion, carrot, celery, bouquet garni and peppercorns. Add 1.8 litres (3 pints) cold water and bring slowly to the boil.

❷ Reduce the heat and simmer the stock very gently for 3 hours, skimming the surface from time to time if necessary.

❸ Strain the stock through a large sieve, preferably a conical one, and leave to cool. Don't press or squeeze the juice out of the vegetables or the stock will be cloudy.

❹ Leave the stock to cool completely, then chill. Remove any layer of fat that might have set on the surface before use.

Lamb stock

Stock made with lamb is less versatile than beef and chicken stock because of its distinctive flavour. If you have plenty of bones, though, it's well worth making some for lamb dishes. Roast the bones first, then follow the recipe for beef stock, simmering the stock for just 1½ hours.

Veal stock

Use the same method as for beef stock, using raw bones for a lighter, general-purpose stock. Veal stock usually jellies naturally, so it can be used for pâtés.

Chicken stock

Ideally, chicken stock is made using a raw carcass, either from the butcher or from a chicken you've jointed for a recipe. However, don't throw away a cooked carcass because it will make an acceptable, well-flavoured stock, although it might be cloudy.

Preparation time 10 minutes
Cooking time 1½ hours
Makes about 1 litre (1¾ pints)

1 large chicken carcass, plus any trimmings and giblets, except the liver, if available
1 onion, quartered
1 celery stick, roughly chopped
1 bouquet garni or 3 bay leaves
1 teaspoon black peppercorns

❶ Put all the ingredients into a heavy-based saucepan and add 1.8 litres (3 pints) cold water.

❷ Make the stock following the recipe for Beef Stock (see above), but simmer it for just 1½ hours.

Vegetable stock

You can use almost any mixture of vegetables, but they must be really fresh. Make sure you include some onion, but omit vegetables with strong flavours, such as cabbage, and starchy ones, like potatoes, which will make the stock cloudy. For a dark stock leave the skins on the onions and use plenty of mushrooms.

Preparation time 10 minutes
Cooking time 45 minutes
Makes about 1 litre (1¾ pints)

1 tablespoon sunflower oil
2 onions, roughly chopped
2 carrots, roughly chopped
2 celery sticks, roughly chopped
500 g (1 lb) mixture other vegetables, such as parsnips, fennel, leeks, courgettes, mushrooms and tomatoes

❶ Heat the oil in a large, heavy-based saucepan and gently fry all the vegetables for 5 minutes.

❷ Add 1 litre (1¾ pints) cold water, then follow the method for Beef Stock (see opposite), simmering the stock for just 40 minutes.

Fish stock

Don't use oily fish in a stock: it will make it greasy and give an overpoweringly strong flavour. Fish stock needs much less cooking than meat stocks, so take care not to overcook it or its flavour will deteriorate.

Preparation time 5 minutes
Cooking time 25 minutes
Makes about 1 litre (1¾ pints)

25 g (1 oz) butter
3 shallots, roughly chopped
1 small leek, roughly chopped
1 celery stick or piece of fennel, roughly chopped
1 kg (2 lb) white fish or shellfish bones, heads and trimmings
150 ml (¼ pint) dry white wine
several parsley stalks
½ lemon, sliced
1 teaspoon black or white peppercorns

❶ Melt the butter in a large, heavy-based saucepan until bubbling. Add all the vegetables. Gently fry for 5 minutes to soften them slightly without browning.

❷ Add the fish bones, wine, parsley, lemon slices, peppercorns and 1 litre (1¾ pints) cold water.

❸ Follow the method for Beef Stock (see opposite), simmering the stock for just 20 minutes.

Basic sauce recipes

The following sauces are used in many recipes throughout the book and you will find that mastering the basic techniques will make them easy to adapt and enhance with additional flavours, when required.

Béchamel sauce

This sauce features in so many dishes that it's worth getting it just right. It can be spooned over vegetables, gratin style, layered in baked dishes like lasagne, or tossed with pasta, and with extra flavourings, it can be transformed into different sauces. This quantity makes enough for four servings as an accompaniment.

Preparation time 10 minutes, plus infusing
Cooking time 10 minutes
Serves 4

300 ml (½ pint) full-cream milk
½ small onion
1 bay leaf
½ teaspoon peppercorns
3–4 parsley stalks
15 g (½ oz) butter
15 g (½ oz) plain flour
freshly grated nutmeg
salt and pepper

❶ Put the milk into a saucepan with the onion, bay leaf, peppercorns and parsley stalks and bring almost to the boil. Remove the pan from the heat and leave to infuse for 20 minutes. Strain the milk through a sieve into a jug.

❷ Melt the butter in a heavy-based saucepan until bubbling. Tip in the flour and stir quickly to combine. Cook the mixture gently, stirring constantly with a wooden spoon, for 1–2 minutes to make a smooth, pale roux.

❸ Remove the pan from the heat and gradually whisk in the warm milk, stirring constantly until the sauce is completely smooth. Return the pan to a moderate heat and cook, stirring, until the sauce comes to the boil.

❹ Reduce the heat to low and continue to cook the sauce for about 5 minutes, stirring frequently until it is smooth and glossy and thinly coats the back of the spoon. Season to taste with salt, pepper and plenty of freshly grated nutmeg.

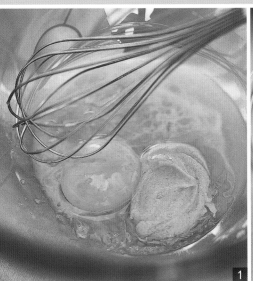

Mayonnaise

Mayonnaise is the most versatile chilled sauce. It is delicious as it is, or it can be used as a base for many tasty variations. Make it with sunflower or light olive oil but avoid very strong olive oils as their flavour can be too overpowering. Good-quality egg yolks, preferably organic ones, will also give the best results.

Preparation time 10 minutes
Serves 6–8

2 egg yolks
2 teaspoons Dijon mustard
1–2 tablespoons white wine vinegar
250 ml (8 fl oz) oil
salt and pepper

1. Put the egg yolks, mustard, 1 tablespoon vinegar and a little salt and pepper in a large bowl and whisk lightly with a balloon whisk to combine.

2. Whisking continuously, start adding the oil, a few drops at a time, until the sauce starts to thicken.

3. Gradually add the remaining oil in a very thin, steady stream until the mayonnaise is thick and glossy. Don't add the oil too quickly or the mayonnaise might start to separate. If this happens, try whisking in 1 tablespoon warm water. If the mixture curdles completely, whisk another egg yolk in a separate bowl and gradually whisk it into the curdled sauce.

4. Check the seasoning, adding a little more vinegar if the sauce tastes bland. Mayonnaise can be kept, covered, in the refrigerator for up to 2 days.

Hollandaise sauce

Hollandaise is a thick, velvety sauce. It perfects a springtime starter, generously spooned over fresh asparagus spears or new potatoes, broccoli, pan-fried fish or egg dishes. It requires just a little patience and needs to be made within about half an hour of serving.

Preparation time 10 minutes
Cooking time 10 minutes
Serves 6

2 tablespoons white wine vinegar
1 bay leaf
½ teaspoon black peppercorns
3 egg yolks
200 g (7 oz) unsalted butter, softened and cut into
1 cm (½ inch) cubes
salt and pepper

1 Put the vinegar, bay leaf, peppercorns and 1 tablespoon water in a small, heavy-based saucepan. Heat until bubbling and simmer until the liquid has reduced by half.

2 Heat a medium-sized pan containing about 5 cm (2 inches) of water until simmering. Put the egg yolks in a heatproof bowl that sits comfortably over the pan without the base touching the water. Strain the vinegar mixture into the yolks and whisk lightly to combine.

3 Whisk in a cube of butter. As soon as it has melted into the sauce, add another cube and whisk again until absorbed. Continue adding the remaining butter, one cube at a time, until the sauce is thick and glossy. Check the flavour and season with salt and pepper.

Roasted tomato sauce

This sauce, a fabulous partner to so many fish dishes, is worth making only if really ripe, flavoursome fresh tomatoes are available; otherwise, use a couple of cans of chopped tomatoes.

Preparation time 10 minutes
Cooking time 50 minutes
Makes 750 ml (1¼ pints)

1 kg (2 lb) very ripe tomatoes
4 tablespoons olive oil
1 teaspoon caster sugar
1 onion, finely chopped
4 garlic cloves, crushed
2 tablespoons chopped oregano
salt and pepper

1 Halve the tomatoes and arrange them, cut sides up, in a large, shallow, ovenproof dish or roasting tin.

2 Drizzle with 2 tablespoons of the oil, the sugar and seasoning. Roast in a preheated oven, 200°C (400°F), Gas Mark 6, for 40 minutes or until the tomatoes are soft and beginning to colour.

3 Gently fry the onion in the remaining oil in a saucepan for about 10 minutes or until it is soft, adding the garlic for the last couple of minutes.

4 Blend the tomatoes in a food processor or blender and add to the pan with the oregano. Cook gently for 5–10 minutes or until slightly thickened. Check the seasoning and serve.

Pasta

Making your own pasta may seem a little daunting at first, but the whole process is very satisfying and addictive! Ensure that you use top-quality, organic free-range eggs and invest in a decent pasta machine.

Basic pasta dough

This quantity is sufficient for four servings as part of a meal. If you are making stuffed pasta, when there is more wastage, you can increase the ingredients to 300 g (10 oz) flour and 3 large eggs. If you can't get hold of pasta '00' flour use strong white bread flour instead.

Preparation time 15 minutes, plus standing, rolling and shaping
Serves 4 as a main course, 6–8 as a starter

200 g (7 oz) '00' grade flour, plus extra for dusting
2 large eggs

1. Tip the flour on to the work surface and make a well in the centre. (Working directly on the work surface is the traditional and easiest way of mixing pasta dough, but if you feel uncertain about working on the surface use a mixing bowl.) Break the eggs into the well. Beat the eggs lightly with a fork and, as you beat, gradually start to blend the flour into the eggs.

2. When the eggs are thickened with flour, push the rest of the flour over the eggs and mix the whole lot together to make a crumbly paste using your fingertips.

3. Continue to work the mixture to a dough, sprinkling in more flour if the dough starts sticking to the surface. Pasta dough should feel firmer and more compact than bread or pastry dough but not so firm that it's leathery and unsupple.

4. Knead the dough until it is smooth and elastic, then wrap it in clingfilm and leave to stand at room temperature for 20 minutes. This will relax the dough and make it easier to roll and shape.

Rolling out the dough

Pasta dough has to be rolled out before it can be shaped, either by hand or machine. Once you've made your chosen pasta it can be stored in the refrigerator for a few hours, or frozen or dried for longer storage.

Line two or three baking sheets or trays with tea towels or kitchen paper and lightly dust them with flour. Divide the dough into six wedges (or 8–10 wedges if you are working with a larger quantity).

Using a pasta machine

Flatten a piece of dough into an oval shape that's slightly narrower than the machine rollers and dust generously with flour. Set the machine to its widest setting and roll the pasta through the machine. Reset the machine to a slightly narrower setting, fold the pasta in half lengthways, dust with flour and run it through again. Roll the pasta through the machine once or twice more, each time setting the machine to a narrower setting, until it is 1–2 mm (about $\frac{1}{16}$ inch) thick. (You probably won't need to go to the narrowest setting on the machine because the pasta will be too thin to use.) If necessary, cut the pasta lengths in half to make them more manageable. Lay the rolled sheets on the lined baking sheets or trays while rolling the remainder.

Shaping by hand

Dust the dough, work surface and rolling pin with flour and roll out the dough as thinly as possible.

Flavoured pasta

Flavoured pastas can be bought fresh or dried, or made at home. The following flavour variations are used for a 200 g (7 oz) quantity of flour.

Herb

Finely chop 25 g (1 oz) of a single herb or mixed herbs. Flat leaf parsley, dill, fennel, coriander, basil, thyme and tarragon are all suitable, but make sure they're thoroughly dry before chopping. Whisk into the eggs before working in the flour.

Mushroom

Cover 15 g ($\frac{1}{2}$ oz) dried porcini mushrooms with boiling water and leave for 15 minutes. Drain, reserving 2 teaspoons of the juice. Blend the mushrooms and reserved juice in a food processor to make a paste and mix with the eggs before working in the flour. Add extra flour if the dough feels sticky.

Spinach

Cook 100 g ($3\frac{1}{2}$ oz) spinach leaves in a saucepan with a splash of water until wilted. Drain and squeeze the spinach dry in your hands to remove as much moisture as possible. Dry further by pressing between several sheets of kitchen paper. Blend in a food processor with one of the eggs, then mix with the remaining egg and make as for plain pasta. The dough will be stickier than a plain pasta dough because of the moisture in the spinach, so you'll need to work in extra flour.

Tomato

Add 2 tablespoons sun-dried tomato paste to the eggs before working in the flour. Add a little extra flour when kneading if the dough feels sticky.

Making ravioli

Ravioli is usually cut to about 5 cm (2 inch) squares, but you can experiment with mini ravioli – about 3 cm (1¼ inches) square, large ones – about 8.5 cm (3½ inches) square – or rounds (see below). Special ravioli tins are useful for making a large amount of ravioli, but it's really very easy, and rewarding, to make ravioli by hand.

Put a pasta sheet on a floured work surface. Place scant teaspoonfuls of the filling in a line, at 2.5 cm (1 inch) intervals, down the length of the dough and flatten them slightly. If the pasta is wide enough, add more spoonfuls of filling, making sure there is a 2.5 cm (1 inch) gap between each. Using a pastry brush with a little water, lightly brush the pasta all around the piles of filling. Loosely lay another sheet of pasta on top. Working from one end, press the dough down between the mounds, sealing the filling firmly and excluding all the air. Use a knife or ravioli cutter to cut the ravioli into squares between the mounds. Transfer to floured tea towels or paper while you make the remainder.

Make round ravioli as above but cut out rounds using a plain or fluted ravioli or biscuit cutter.

TIP COOKING FRESH PASTA

Fresh pasta should be cooked in a large saucepan of boiling water for between 2 and 3 minutes, or until al dente (firm to the bite). Stir the pasta to prevent it sticking and don't cover the pan. If you dry the pasta first (over pasta drying racks), allow approximately 5 minutes cooking time. Drain well and serve immediately with a sauce.

Making tagliatelle

Cut the sheets of pasta to about 30 cm (12 inches) in length to make them more manageable. Flour the pasta and fold it over several times. Cut the pasta into strips about 5–10 mm (¼–½ inch) wide. Unroll the pasta to separate the layers. Alternatively, shape the pasta by running it through the tagliatelle cutter of the pasta machine

Gnocchi

This is not a true pasta but shares many similarities in the way it is prepared and cooked. It can be made several hours in advance if stored in the refrigerator.

Preparation time 30 minutes
Cooking time 45 minutes
Serves 4

750 g (1½ lb) medium, floury potatoes
40 g (1½ oz) Parmesan cheese, grated
125–150 g (4–5 oz) plain flour
salt

1. Put the potatoes, whole and unpeeled, in a saucepan and cover with water. Bring to the boil and boil for about 40 minutes until tender. (Try not to pierce them too often, or they will absorb too much water.) Drain and peel the potatoes when they are cool enough to handle. Return the potatoes to a cleaned pan and mash until smooth, then beat in the Parmesan and a little salt. Add 100 g (3½ oz) of the flour, beating with a wooden spoon until smooth.

2. When the mixture becomes too dry to mix, turn it out and knead in a little more flour with your hands. Stop working in the flour when the mixture makes a soft dough that's only slightly sticky. Divide into 4 and roll each under the palms of your hands to a long rope about 1.5 cm (¾ inch) thick. Cut into pieces 2.5 cm (1 inch) long.

3. Take a piece of gnocchi and press it on the tines of a floured fork, pressing an indentation into the other side with your finger and rolling the gnocchi slightly to make it into a curved shape. Repeat with the remaining pieces.

4. Bring a large saucepan of salted water to the boil and boil the gnocchi, in batches, for about 2 minutes until they rise to the surface. Lift out the gnocchi with a slotted spoon and drain thoroughly.

Meat

Tenderness and flavour are the essence of good meat. Whenever possible, look for organically reared produce from small or local suppliers where these qualities far outshine those of cheaper, mass-produced cuts.

The most practical answer to sourcing good meat is to find a butcher who cares about the quality of the meat he sells and where it comes from.

Bright red flesh is not necessarily a sign of quality. A deep, dark red flesh usually shows that the meat has been hung properly. Look for a smooth outer layer of fat that is not too thick and a light marbling of fat through the lean flesh. Choose well-trimmed meat and steaks and chops that are of an even thickness. Never buy prepacked meat that has a grey tinge.

Beef

For the best flavour and texture beef should be hung after slaughter for at least two weeks. During this time enzymes and bacteria contained in the meat break down the fibres, making it more tender, deepening the colour and giving it time to develop flavour. Choose beef that is marbled with streaks of fat, which helps it stay succulent.

Best cuts for roasting

Fore rib (also available boned and rolled); wing rib (can also be cut into porterhouse steaks); sirloin (sold on the bone or boned and rolled); fillet (tenderloin, which is best cooked rare as it tends to dry out).

Best cuts for pot-roasting and braising

Top rump (thick flank, which can also be thinly sliced for frying or stir-frying); topside (round steak); silverside (can be bought salted and spiced) and brisket (sold boned and rolled and often salted).

Best cuts for frying and grilling

Fillet steak (if cut from the thin end, known as filets mignons; tournedos, if taken from further up the fillet; and chateaubriand from the thickest end of a large fillet and a hefty steak usually serving two). Also, sirloin steak and entrecôte steak (from the middle of the sirloin); rump steak (has a firmer texture than sirloin); T-bone steak; porterhouse steak and rib-eye steak.

Best cuts for slow cooking

Chuck (blade, sold sliced or cubed for braising, stewing and pies); short ribs (best slowly braised so the meat falls off the bone); neck and clod (a cheaper cut for stewing and good for the stock pot); flank (often trimmed and made into mince); skirt (flank steak), shin (foreleg) and leg (hock, hough). Also, minced beef (look for a good, rich colour, which denotes less fat); oxtail, ox kidney and ox liver (perfect for pâtés).

Veal

This meat comes from milk-fed calves, which are slaughtered when they are between 8 and 12 weeks old, or from slightly older (four to five months old), grass-fed calves. All veal should be pale and moist-looking without any redness. The meat should be very lean with a little marbling of fat similar in colour to the flesh.

Best cuts for roasting

Leg (best roasted under a layer of fat bacon, or pot-roasted with vegetables to counteract dryness); loin (cooked on the bone or boned and rolled).

Best cuts for frying and grilling
Escalopes (thin steaks usually cut from the fillet end of the leg, often pounded). Also, tenderloin (chunky slices or medallions) and loin chops.

Best cuts for pot-roasting, braising and stewing
Middle neck (sold as cutlets); chump (sold boned and rolled for slow cooking); shoulder/breast (boned and rolled for pot-roasting); shin; minced veal and liver.

Lamb
The texture and flavour of lamb for cooking depends largely on the age of the animal at slaughter. Young lamb (under one year) is considered the best, although older meat has as much, if not more, flavour. Older meats, which require gentler cooking, are known as hoggit (over one year old) or mutton (two to three years old).

Best cuts for roasting
Leg (sold boned or part-boned, and sometimes butterflied, which cooks more quickly); chump, shoulder (ballotines are available boned and stuffed), rack of lamb (a joint of seven or eight ribs) and loin (on the bone, boned and rolled).

Best cuts for grilling, frying and barbecuing
Chops; cutlets (allow three per person); noisettes (boned and rolled rack of lamb); leg steaks; chump chops; neck fillet (tenderloin); liver and kidneys.

Best cuts for stewing and braising
Scrag (more bone, gristle and fat than other cuts but plenty of flavour so good for soups and stews); breast, middle neck and minced lamb.

Pork
The cheapest of the mainstream meats, pork has, with chicken, suffered from intensive farming, resulting in plump meat that is not hung and has little flavour. Most pigs are slaughtered when they are several months old (porkers), except for suckling pig, popular in Spain, where pigs are slaughtered at three to eight weeks.

Best cuts for roasting and pot-roasting
Leg (contains less fat than other cuts of pork, so take extra care when cooking to prevent it from drying out); loin (delicious on or off the bone); chump end; and shoulder (blade).

Best cuts for frying, grilling and barbecuing
Loin chops, chump chops and tenderloin (fillet), which can be sliced into medallions for grilling or frying.

Best cuts for slow cooking
Hand and spring (a cheaper cut from the front legs often cut up for stewing and mince); spare ribs; belly (fatty, but full flavoured); diced or pie pork (good for curries, pies, casseroles and kebabs); minced pork (from cheaper cuts); liver and kidneys.

Ham
Most ham comes from the pig's hind legs. In its raw, cured state, this is known as gammon; when cooked, it is known as ham. Ready-cooked hams can be bought whole or sliced. Those bought for home cooking should be soaked for at least 24 hours (or up to several days if large). Pork can also be cured for eating uncooked and thinly sliced. Italian prosciutto is widely known, and Parma ham is considered the best. These are cured and then air-dried for several months.

Bacon
Smoked or unsmoked (green) bacon can be bought in the piece or sliced. Flavoursome belly pork is used for bacons such as pancetta, speck, tocino or streaky. Leaner cuts come from meatier parts of the pig, such as the back. All bacon is cooked before being eaten.

Poultry

Once reserved for special occasions, poultry, especially chicken, has become one of the most widely available and widely eaten of meats. For best flavour, avoid battery-farmed birds.

Chicken

Chicken is one of the most versatile meats. Its lean texture and relatively mild flavour make it incredibly 'useful' to cook with, from a simple roast to hot, spicy, aromatic dishes.

A specific farm or breed label is a good guide to quality and, although better-quality birds are inevitably more expensive, you can still be quite thrifty with a decent chicken. Buy a large one and you can serve it roasted one day and tossed with a salad the next or made into sandwich fillings or combined with a sauce to accompany a pasta dish. The bones, trimmings and giblets can be made into a delicious stock base for soup, with any leftover meat and plenty of vegetables added to make a third meal.

Poussins and yellow-fleshed, corn-fed chickens are also subject to intensive farming, so look for free-range or organic labels on the packs when buying.

Duck

Though richly flavoured, duck contains a high percentage of fat. Most meat is on the breast fillets, but as a guide, a duck weighing 2.5 kg (5 lb) will serve four people. Always prick the skin with a skewer before roasting to let the fat melt out and roast the bird on a rack over the roasting tin. Some duck are specially reared for Chinese recipes, such as Peking duck, and are labelled accordingly.

Goose

There is actually little meat per kilo (pound) on an oven-ready goose, because much of it is fat that's cooked off during roasting. A 5–6 kg (10–12 lb) goose will serve up to ten people. Rich in flavour, goose is usually partnered with tangy, light stuffings and accompaniments such as apples, raisins and chestnuts. Before roasting, prick the skin with a skewer to let the fat melt out and pull out the lumps of fat in the cavity. Roast the goose and the removed layer of fat on a rack over the roasting tin.

The huge amount of valuable fat that collects in the tin below the bird during roasting can be poured off and stored in the refrigerator for dripping. Use it spread on bread, for roasting potatoes or making cassoulets and confits.

Guinea fowl

Guinea fowl, which tastes like slightly gamey chicken, can be used instead of chicken when you are looking for something more unusual. As with chicken, the flavour varies greatly between intensively farmed and free-range birds.

Turkey

Although traditionally served on festive occasions, turkey is always a lean and economical choice for the cook all year-round. Although usually sold as whole birds, the breast meat can be sold separately as a piece, in steaks or in strips for stir-frying. It makes a suitable substitute for chicken in most spicy dishes. Allow 350 g (11½ oz) for each person when you are buying a whole turkey for roasting.

Trussing

Trussing poultry helps maintain a good shape during roasting and prevents the leg meat from drying out. Remove any plastic trussing and fill the cavity with stuffing, if used. Stretch the neck flap under the bird and fold back the wing tips to hold the flap in place. Position the bird with the neck cavity facing you and pull a long piece of string under the bird, bringing the ends up on either side between the legs and wings. Take the string back between the legs and breasts and hook it under the ends of each drumstick, bringing them around the outside of the drumsticks. Firmly tie the ends together over the cavity. Loop the ends under the parson's nose and tie together once more.

Jointing chicken and guinea fowl

Cut off the legs through the joints, bending the legs back as you work so the leg sockets are more visible. Place the legs, skin side down, on the board and cut the drumstick from the thigh. (This will be easier if you bend the legs back and forth so that you can see more clearly where the joint is.) Make a cut down one side of the breastbone, then ease the breast meat away from the bone, keeping the knife as close to the bone as possible to avoid wastage. Cut through the joint where the wing is attached. Repeat on the other side. Cut the wings from the breast meat, taking a little of the breast meat with it. If liked, halve each breast widthways.

Skewering a duck or goose

Place the bird, breast side down, on a board and prick it all over with a fine skewer so the fat can run out during roasting. For presentation, avoid pricking the breast area.

Checking the bird is cooked

Chicken, turkey and guinea fowl must always be thoroughly cooked through. To make sure they are cooked properly, push a skewer through the thickest part of the thigh. If the juices run clear, the bird is cooked. If they are still pink return the bird to the oven for a little longer.

Spatchcocking

Small chickens, poussins and game birds can be spatchcocked, which involves splitting and flattening them to make it easier to grill or barbecue them. Remove any trussing from the bird. Use kitchen scissors or poultry shears to cut off the wing tips, then cut through the bony meat on either side of the backbone. Discard the backbone and cut the wishbone in half. Flatten the bird by pushing down on the breastbone with the heel of your hand – this will break the breastbone. You can retain the flattened shape of larger birds by pushing a couple of long skewers horizontally through the wings and breasts. The meat can be marinated before cooking.

Game and other meats

Furred or feathered, game is becoming more popular as an interesting and healthy alternative to other meats. Most game is protected by law to prevent animals from being over-hunted and to allow for the rearing of their young.

Goat

Similar in flavour to lamb, goat can be a good substitute in spicy casseroles and stews. You may need to order it from a specialist supplier.

Grouse

The most prized and most expensive of the game birds, grouse has a relatively short season. Younger grouse taste best simply roasted with a covering of bacon to keep them moist. Older birds benefit from marinating or are added to game pies and casseroles. Allow one bird per serving.

Hare

Leverets (hares under a year old) are the most tender and delicious, after which they start to toughen so may need longer cooking. Darker meat than rabbit, hare should be hung for several days before use. Dry in texture, it is best marinated or wrapped in fat before slow roasting or casseroling.

Ostrich

A lean and tender alternative to mainstream meats, ostrich is available from specialist suppliers. Prime ostrich steaks can be pan-fried, just as you would cook beef, while tougher cuts are best added to stews and casseroles.

Partridge

More delicate than most birds, partridge is best accompanied with similarly delicate flavourings. Like pigeon, most of the meat is on the breasts and the rest of the bird should be consigned to making flavoursome stock. Allow one bird per serving.

Pheasant

Often bought as a brace, consisting of the slightly larger male and smaller, juicier female. A pheasant that has not been hung tastes marginally more gamey than a chicken, while a pheasant that has been hung for several weeks will have an extremely strong flavour. Young pheasant can be wrapped in bacon and roasted, while older birds are best pot-roasted or used in pies and casseroles.

Pigeon

Pigeon has a richly flavoured, deep red flesh that toughens up on older birds and can be tenderized by marinating in red wine. Remove the breasts for cooking and use the rest of the carcass for well-flavoured stock. Allow one or two birds per serving.

Quail

Small and mildly flavoured, quail is usually served whole, sometimes stuffed or with sauces using ingredients such as raisins, sherry and crème fraîche. In some Mediterranean countries they are served wrapped in vine leaves. Allow two per portion unless really large.

Rabbit

The strength of flavour will depend on the animal's age and whether it is wild or farmed. Rabbit is best eaten when it is not too young, because the flavour will not

have had time to develop, but it can be eaten without hanging first. Widely used in Spanish cooking, rabbit can be roasted with olive oil and herbs or cooked with wine or garlic. Rabbit pie is a traditional country speciality, flavoured with robust ingredients like bacon and mustard. An average-sized rabbit comfortably serves two people.

Venison

Venison is the meat taken from roe, fallow or red deer and is available both wild and farmed. The hanging time determines the 'gaminess' of the flavour, and this can range from several days to up to three weeks. Saddle, loin and leg (haunch) are choice cuts for roasting, while other more sinewy parts are sold diced for pâtés, pies and casseroles. Venison sausages are also widely available.

Buy meat that is dark and close grained. Venison has a tendency to dryness and can benefit from marinating prior to cooking.

Wild boar

Boar, stronger tasting than pork but leaner, is best eaten young, and the meat is well suited to fruity accompaniments, such as lemons, junipers, chestnuts and peppers. The flesh should be dark with little fat. If young, hanging will tenderize the flesh, but other meat needs marinating, too – red wine complements the rich flavour. Legs and saddle can be roasted, baste the meat frequently and cover with a layer of fat, such as bacon; other cuts can be grilled, fried or braised. Boar must be cooked through before eating.

Preparing game birds for roasting

To prepare a young bird for a simple roast, remove any stray feathers (tweezers may be required for removing small pin feathers along the backbone) and wash the cavity thoroughly before seasoning inside and out. Tuck herbs, such as rosemary, sage, tarragon, parsley or thyme, into the cavity and lay strips of fat bacon over the breast (known as barding). To help tenderize the meat you can marinate it in red or white wine. Roast in a hot oven, 200°C (400°F), Gas Mark 6, for between 15 and 45 minutes, depending on the size of the bird. Test by piercing the flesh between thigh and breast to see if the bird is cooked – the bird is cooked if the juices run clear.

Removing breast meat

For small birds, such as partridge and pigeon, use a sharp knife to cut down one side of the breastbone and carefully ease the meat away. Remove the skin.

Cooking meat

There are many cuts of meat available, and all are suited to different cooking methods and times. Some cuts are suited to fast cooking, such as grilling or frying, whereas others benefit from slow cooking in sauces and stews.

The more expensive cuts of meat, taken from the least exercised parts of the body (usually the hindquarters), can be cooked fast, hot and dry – by roasting, grilling, frying and barbecuing, for example. Tougher cuts, usually from the most exercised parts of the body (the forequarters), are best cooked gently and slowly, partially or fully immersed in liquid.

Storing

Most meats, especially larger pieces, will keep well in the refrigerator for several days. The exceptions are poultry, minced meat and offal, which should be cooked as soon as possible after purchase. Never leave meat in its original supermarket packaging because it cannot breathe and will spoil more quickly. All meat should be loosened from its wrapping, particularly if it

is in plastic, then transferred to a plate and lightly covered so that air can circulate. Store meat in the coldest part of the refrigerator. Most meats freeze well.

Roasting

Roast choice tender cuts on or off the bone, with or without stuffing. Sear a joint for roasting in oil first (in hot fat in the roasting tin on the hob or in a very hot oven) before you reduce the temperature to a moderate heat that will penetrate to the centre without burning the outside. Roasting times vary, depending on the type of meat, size and cut. If time allows, cook the meat from room temperature so that it heats through quickly.

Frying

Individual portions of tender meat – steak, escalopes and chops, for example – can be fried quickly so they are appetizingly browned on the outside and, for most people's tastes, still pink in the middle. Use a good-quality, sturdy pan and don't cram in too many pieces at once or the meat will steam. Season on both sides first and get the oil or butter sizzling hot before you add the meat. Once cooked, the flavoursome residue and juices in the pan can be deglazed (see page 36).

ROASTING TIMES FOR MEATS

Unless the recipe states otherwise, roast the joint at 220°C (425°F), Gas Mark 7, for 15 minutes, then reduce the oven temperature to 180°C (350°F), Gas Mark 4, and cook for the following times. The heat indications show the internal meat temperature.

Beef

(rare)	10 minutes per 500 g (1 lb)	45°C (113°F)
(medium)	15 minutes per 500 g (1 lb)	60°C (140°F)
(well done)	20 minutes per 500 g (1 lb)	75°C (167°F)

Veal

	15 minutes per 500 g (1 lb)	70°C (158°F)

Lamb

(rare)	10 minutes per 500 g (1 lb)	45°C (113°F)
(medium)	15 minutes per 500 g (1 lb)	60°C (140°F)
(well done)	20 minutes per 500 g (1 lb)	75°C (167°F)

Pork

	25–30 minutes per 500 g (1 lb)	75°C (167°F)

Chicken does not need initial cooking at a high temperature; allow 30 minutes per 500 g (1 lb) at 190°C (375°F), Gas Mark 5.

COOKING TIMES FOR STEAKS

The following times are for steaks 2 cm (¾ inch) thick.

- Blue Cook very briefly on each side until seared but completely rare in the centre.

- Rare 1½ minutes each side until heated through but very pink in the centre.

- Medium rare 2½ minutes each side or until most of the steak is cooked with just a thin band of pink running through the centre.

- Medium to well done 5 minutes on each side until completely cooked through but still moist.

Stir-frying

Meat for stir-frying should be cut into thin strips or slices and lightly seasoned. A wok is ideal so that you can give the meat a good stir without it falling out of the pan. Make sure that the fat is really hot before you add the meat and fry in small quantities if you're cooking a lot. Always stir-fry the meat before you add vegetables to the pan.

Pot-roasting and braising

Joints of meat that tend to be tough can be pot-roasted or braised on or off the bone, with or without stuffing. This is an excellent cooking method that allows flavours to mingle, and because the cooking juices are so delicious it means you don't have to make a sauce or gravy. First, sear the joint on all sides in butter or oil, then simmer with a little stock, wine or beer and vegetables, herbs or spices, before cooking in the oven or on the hob. This method can also be used for choice cuts, such as rolled loin of pork, which leaves you free to get on with other things, confident that the gentle cooking process won't dry out or overcook the meat.

Stewing and casseroling

These cooking methods are very similar. Generally, stews are cooked on a hob and casseroles in an oven, although stews can be cooked in an oven and left unattended. It's the best way to transform cheaper cuts of meat into fabulously tender dishes, and some stews will really benefit from cooking one day and then reheating the next. The key to success is thoroughly frying off the meat before you begin stewing.

Grilling

For straightforward, clean and easy cooking, grilling under an overhead grill is perfect, using the meat's integral fat to prevent it from drying out and doing away with the need for additional fat. Lightly season the meat before cooking and preheat the grill. Chargrilling is usually done on a gas- or electric-powered grill that imitates barbecuing. A ridged grill pan, preheated over the hob, is another very effective way of grilling (see page 13).

Poaching

Some meats, such as a joint of bacon, a brisket of beef or breast fillets of chicken, can be cooked gently in water with additional vegetables and herbs so they retain maximum moisture. The poaching liquid can then be used in a sauce. It's vital that once the liquid has reached simmering point it's turned down to its lowest setting so the meat is cooked gently. Meat that has been boiled for a long time will remain tough.

Frying off

If you're making a casserole or stew, frying off produces a good flavour and rich colour. Make sure the meat is thoroughly dry first and, if necessary, is floured and/or seasoned with salt and pepper (see below). Heat the fat in a sturdy, heavy-based frying pan and add a batch of the meat. Don't try to fry off too much at once. The chunks of meat need plenty of space around them or they'll steam in their own juice. Use a wooden spatula to turn the meat once or twice during frying until it is deeply browned. Drain and transfer the meat with a slotted spoon while you fry the remainder.

Searing joints

Larger pieces of meat are usually seared before roasting or pot-roasting to add colour and keep in all the flavour. Pat the meat dry with kitchen paper if it's moist and season with salt and pepper (see below). Heat the fat in a heavy-based frying pan or roasting tin and sear the meat thoroughly until browned.

Flouring meat

Meat is sometimes floured before frying, which gives a good colour and thickens the cooking liquid. Make sure the meat is really dry first, patting it dry on kitchen paper if necessary. Season the flour with a little salt and pepper and toss the meat in it until it is lightly dusted all over.

Preparing escalopes

Veal escalopes are used widely in Italian cooking and can be prepared from leg steaks. Place each slice between two sheets of clingfilm and beat the meat until it is flattened with a rolling pin or meat mallet to tenderize it as thoroughly as possible.

Deglazing

After frying or roasting meat there's plenty of flavour left in the pan or tin to form the base of a good sauce or gravy. Pour a little wine or stock into the pan and cook over the hob, stirring with a wooden spatula as you scrape up the pan residue. If you're making gravy, the mixture can bubble for a few minutes so the liquid reduces and the flavour intensifies.

Marinating

Marinades have only a minimal effect as meat tenderizers. Even acid ingredients, like lemon or orange juice and vinegar, cannot get through to the centre of the meat, and wine can sometimes even draw out moisture, resulting in a tougher texture. Marinades, wet or dry, are much better as flavour enhancers, penetrating meat with delicious aromatic ingredients,

such as garlic, herbs and spices. They also give you an opportunity to prepare a dish in advance, perhaps first thing in the day, so it's ready for cooking, effortlessly, in the evening.

Basting

Traditionally, many meats, particularly roast joints, are basted (flooded with the pan juices), several times during cooking. This method has the most beneficial effects on chicken, which develops a crisper, tastier skin as a result.

Using a meat thermometer

A meat thermometer enables you to detect whether a roasted joint has reached the right temperature and therefore has had the right amount of cooking. Insert the point of the thermometer into the thickest part of the joint, away from the bone (which would affect the reading), and leave it for 20–30 seconds. For pork, which must be served cooked through, it should read 70–75°C (158–167°F). For lamb and beef it can range from 45°C (113°F) for very rare, through to 75°C (167°F) for well done.

Resting meat

Resting a joint of meat after cooking is essential. This enables the muscle fibres to relax after cooking, making the meat more tender and easier to carve. Transfer the meat to a serving platter, cover with foil and leave for 20–30 minutes, depending on the size of the joint. This gives you plenty of time to make the gravy and finish cooking any vegetables.

Carving

There are recognized ways of carving the different cuts of meat, but the golden rule is to use a good-quality, sharp carving knife, preferably paired with a pronged fork to hold the meat. Making sure the meat has rested first (see above) is essential, as is cutting across the grain of the meat to produce the tenderest slices. Work on a firm, flat surface so that the meat doesn't slip about (a board with a gully round the edges is ideal) and remove any string or skewers first.

Gravy

Good-quality cuts of roasted meat or poultry provide delicious fats and juices for a well-flavoured gravy. After roasting, drain the meat, cover it with foil and make the gravy while the meat rests.

Cooking time 5 minutes
Makes about 600 ml (1 pint)

pan juices from roasted meat
1 tablespoon plain flour (less for a thin gravy)
300–400 ml (10–14 fl oz) liquid (this could be water, drained from the accompanying vegetables; stock; half stock and half water; or half wine and half water)
salt and pepper

1 Tilt the roasting tin and skim off the fat from the surface with a large serving spoon until you are left with the pan juices and just a thin layer of fat.

2 Sprinkle the flour into the tin and stir with a wooden spoon over a moderate heat, scraping up the residue, particularly from around the edges.

3 Gradually pour the liquid into the tin, stirring well until the gravy is thick and glossy. Let the mixture bubble then check the seasoning, adding a little salt and pepper if necessary.

Fish

Among the most inviting aspects of cooking with fish are that it's so fast and so incredibly easy. Fabulous dishes can be made from just a few basic, good-quality ingredients and, of course, by using the freshest fish available.

Today, with the wonderful choice available and the depletion and vulnerability of stocks of some of our favourite fish, we simply must become more experimental with our choices. There are many underrated, delicious fish that deserve a bit of culinary magic, whether for everyday family meals or for smart suppers with friends.

Fluctuations in the availability of fresh fish and the need to support ethical standards in fishing processes mean that as consumers we can make a positive contribution to the future of the fishing industry, primarily in the way we shop. Widen the range of fish you buy – there is, after all, an incredible choice – and be aware of labelling information. This will vary regionally, but does provide useful facts, such as how and where the fish has been caught and whether it has come from a sustainable supply. If you need advice on choosing fish from well-managed, sustainable stocks, ask your local fishmonger.

Buying

One of the slightly frustrating aspects of planning a menu that includes fish is that, unless you're cooking a fish that's widely available, you cannot rely on picking up your exact choice as you might when choosing meat. For this reason, it can be worth ordering two or

three days in advance or going to the fishmonger armed with a couple of different recipe ideas. In addition, fish must be eaten absolutely fresh, so a good supplier is essential. Search out a reliable fishmonger in your area or go to the supermarket that has the freshest-looking display on its fish counter. Make your selection of the freshest choice so that you can do your other shopping while the fishmonger does any preparation for you.

When you are choosing, look for fish with bright eyes – they should not be sunken, dull or cloudy – and a glossy sheen to the skin. The fish, whole or filleted, should look firm and perky rather than limp, grey and ragged. Be particularly careful when you are buying oily fish, such as mackerel, sardines and herrings, because they deteriorate very quickly.

Storing

As far as possible, and particularly with shellfish, you should aim to cook on the day you buy. For most of us, this isn't always practicable, however, and if the fish is really fresh, it'll be fine for the next day. As soon as you get the fish home, gut it (if this has not already been done) and do any other 'messy' preparation, such as scaling. Quickly rinse the whole fish or fillets, removing any traces of blood, but do not soak the fish in water, or you'll end up diluting the flavour. Remove all packaging from prepared fish. Put the fish in a shallow dish, cover it very loosely with clingfilm and store it in the bottom half of the refrigerator.

Shellfish, such as mussels, clams, scallops and oysters, should be cleaned and chilled until you are ready to cook that same day. Cooked shellfish can be stored overnight.

Freezing

Freeze fish with caution. Some raw fish, such as monkfish, salmon and sole, freezes quite well, but other types, including plaice, sea bass, snapper and oily fish, do not. Only freeze fish that is very fresh and keep it for the short term only. A fish that has been in the freezer for three months can end up with a spongy, tough, watery texture.

Preparing shellfish and cephalopods

Shellfish doesn't store as well as other types of fish and is best cooked on the day you buy it. Much of the shellfish available now is already cooked, but if you can buy raw and cook it yourself, the results will be far more rewarding.

Clams and cockles
Although these are less gritty and barnacled than mussels (see below), you will still need to check through clams and cockles carefully, discarding any damaged or stubbornly open shells.

Cuttlefish
Cuttlefish (cephalopods) have chubbier bodies than those of squid, and they have a large, flat bone inside the body. This is most easily removed by cutting down the length of the body and discarding the bone along with the other innards. Otherwise, prepare in the same way as squid (see below).

Mussels
First, wash in cold water to remove all traces of grit. Scrape off any barnacles with a knife and pull away the beards (the seaweed-like threads). As you clean them, check that all the shells are intact, discarding any that are cracked or damaged. Any mussels that are open should close when tapped sharply against the side of the sink. Discard any that don't close.

Prawns
Both raw and cooked prawns are prepared by pinching off the heads and peeling away the shells. If you are serving prawns in a salad, you can leave the tails intact, otherwise remove them. Remove the black, thread-like intestine along the back or underside of larger prawns by making a small cut and pulling it.

Scallops
Usually bought ready prepared, scallops are easy to open if you buy them in their shells. Place the scallop on a chopping board with the flat shell uppermost and insert the blade of a sturdy knife between the two shells on the opposite side to the hinge. Run the knife against the flat top shell so that you can sever the meat from the shell. Discard everything except the coral and white muscle flesh.

Squid
Most squid (also called calamari or inkfish), can be bought ready prepared as the body tubes with or without the heads, or sliced into rings.

If you buy them whole with skin attached, pull away the head and tentacles from the body, then scoop out and discard the contents of the body, including the transparent, plastic-like quill. Pull off and discard the inky skin. This usually rubs off very easily with your fingers. The fins on either side of the body can be removed for cooking separately. Remove the tentacles from the head by cutting just in front of the eyes so that they remain in one piece. Discard the heads. Dry all the pieces thoroughly and chill until ready to cook.

Cooking fish

The fresher the fish, the less you need to do to it to make it taste fabulous. All fish is quick to cook, particularly if you're frying or grilling, so make sure you have any accompaniments ready prepared so that the fish is not kept waiting.

Deep-frying

You don't need an electric deep-fat fryer or even a deep-fat fryer fitted with a special basket, although this does make removing the fish – and chips – much easier. An ordinary large, sturdy saucepan will do, and you will need a large slotted spoon. Never fill the pan more than one-third full with oil and make sure you get the oil to the right temperature before adding any food. Use a thermometer if you have one, cooking fish at 180–190°C (350–375°F), or test the temperature by adding a small cube of bread or a drop of batter to the pan. It should sizzle instantly and turn golden in about 30 seconds.

During cooking, keep an eye on the speed of cooking. If you feel that a piece of battered fish is frying too fast, reduce the heat or turn it off altogether.

Shallow-frying

Fish can be fried to sear in the flavour before it is added to stews or curries, or it can be fried for a simple dish. You will need a good-quality, nonstick frying pan, which is essential for getting a crisp skin and for preventing the fish from sticking to the pan. Shallow-frying gives fish an appetizing golden colour, but take care that you don't overcrowd the pan, which reduces the cooking temperature and steams the fish in its juices. Turn the fish halfway through frying and, if you are serving with its skin on, fry skin side down first.

Grilling

Grilling can be a healthy way to cook fish, but the flavour is usually enhanced by brushing with butter or oil and adding a sprinkling of lemon juice, which will also help to prevent the fish from drying out. If you are using a traditional overhead grill, make sure it's really hot before you start cooking. Make deep slashes in the fish (if it's to be served whole) so that the heat can penetrate the fish quickly and speed up cooking. For convenience, line the grill pan with foil and brush it with butter or oil before cooking so that the fish doesn't stick to the foil. All fish can be grilled, but flat fish are particularly suitable for this method, and a deliciously fresh sole or plaice can be ready to eat in less than 10 minutes.

Confusingly, the term chargrilling is used to describe both the technique of cooking over coals, as on a barbecue, and also in the small, ridged grill pans that are used over the stove. Whatever method you use, chargrilling is great for cooking firm-textured, meaty fish, such as tuna, shark and swordfish. Brush the ridges with oil first and make sure the pan is really hot before you add the fish. Turn once during cooking so that you don't spoil the appetizingly seared marks on the fish. Watch the fish closely to ensure that it doesn't burn or dry out.

Barbecuing

Most fish can be cooked well and fast on a barbecue. Shellfish are delicious cooked this way, as are steaks of tuna, swordfish and shark. Whole fish, including small flat fish and red mullet, sea bass and snapper, also cook well on a barbecue. Oily fish, particularly sardines and herrings, are perfect for barbecuing.

Remember to brush the rack as well as the fish itself with olive oil to prevent the fish from sticking. A sprinkling of fresh herbs and seasoning is all that's needed for additional flavour. You can buy fish-shaped presses that make turning the fish much easier.

Roasting

The technique is similar to that for meat. Get the oven really hot before you add the fish, which can be whole or in fillets, and drizzle it with oil or butter to keep it moist. After roasting, the pan juices can be swirled with reduced fish stock, wine or cream and made into a creamy sauce.

Baking

Baking can be similar to roasting except that the fish might be cooked more slowly and at a lower temperature. Baked fish is often cooked in liquid – stock or wine – and might include vegetables and herbs.

Steaming

This technique has often been thought of as giving rather bland results and only suitable for dieters. Steamed fish can be far from dull, however, particularly if it has been marinated in aromatic ingredients, such as ginger, lime, garlic and spices, so that the flavours seep right into the fish. Fish can be steamed in a bamboo steamer, set over a pan or wok of simmering water, or on a wok rack, tented with foil or a domed lid. Even simpler is to 'oven-steam' fish by laying it on a wire rack in a roasting tin containing a shallow depth of boiled water and covering the whole pan with foil.

Poaching

The traditional method of poaching large whole fish in a court bouillon is not common now, but any pieces of fish lowered into a gently simmering stock or stew is still a form of poaching, as the fish cooks gently in the juices. Keep the pieces of fish quite chunky and make sure the liquid is barely simmering. If it's allowed to boil away frantically, the fish will quickly fall apart.

Pastry

Pastry making is not an esoteric art. It is, rather, a matter of following a set of simple rules, the most important of which is to keep everything cool – hands, head, equipment and ingredients.

Choice of flour

Plain white flour is best for most recipes, giving a light, crisp pastry. Self-raising flour gives a softer, sponge-like texture and should be used for suet crust, which will be heavy without a raising agent. Wholemeal flour, or a mixture of half wholemeal and half white, can be used for shortcrust pastry, but it tends to give heavy crumbly dough, which can be difficult to handle. Puff, flaky or rough puff pastries are usually made with strong plain flour, because its high levels of gluten give the dough more elasticity and strength.

Choice of fat

The type of fat you use will affect the texture as well as the flavour of the pastry. It should be cold, so remove it from the refrigerator shortly before use to make it easier to handle. Butter, preferably unsalted, gives the best colour and flavour, but when it is used on its own it can be rich and oily. Margarine is good for colour but has an inferior flavour to butter; results will depend on the quality. Soft margarine should be used for fork-mix, all-in-one pastry only. Lard, or a good-quality vegetable fat, gives a good short, crumbly texture, but it lacks flavour and colour when used on its own. The best shortcrust pastry is made using equal quantities of butter or margarine with lard or white vegetable fat.

SECRETS OF SUCCESSFUL PASTRY

- Measure the right proportions of fat to flour, according to the type of pastry. For shortcrust pastry use double the weight of flour to fat. Richer short pastries use a higher proportion of fat to flour.

- Unless you are making choux pastry, keep everything, including your hands, as cool as possible.

- When you are rubbing in fats use only the very tips of your fingers to keep the mixture cool. Lift the fingers high and let the crumbs run through them back into the bowl. If you use a food processor pulse the power to make sure that the pastry is not overmixed.

- Avoid handling pastry more than necessary when you are rolling out as this will make it heavy.

- Don't add the liquid all at once. Flours vary in absorbency, and too much liquid can make the pastry heavy.

- Always roll pastry away from you, using light, even pressure and adding as little extra flour as possible – too much can result in tough pastry.

Water

Use as little water as possible to bind the dough. Adding too much water can make the dough sticky and difficult to handle and the cooked pastry tough. Always try to use cold water; in warm weather iced water is ideal. For normal shortcrust pastry you will need about 1 teaspoon of water for each 25 g (1 oz) of flour. Although the amount will vary a little depending on the absorbency of the flour, this is a useful guideline to follow. If you are adding egg or egg yolk use proportionately less water.

Sugar

Some rich pastries, including pâte sucrée (see page 47), include a small amount of sugar to give a crisp texture and golden colour.

Eggs

Egg, usually only the yolk, is used to bind rich pastries. It also adds colour to pastry. Beat it lightly with a fork before adding it to the other ingredients.

Chilling and resting

With the exceptions of choux pastry and suet crust, pastry benefits from resting for about 30 minutes before baking. This reduces shrinkage during cooking and is particularly important for pastries that are handled a great deal during preparation, such as puff pastry. Wrap the pastry in clingfilm to prevent it from drying out and forming a skin (which will crack) and put it in the refrigerator.

Cooking

When you are making pastry it is vital to preheat the oven thoroughly first, particularly for pastries with a high fat content, which should be cooked at a high temperature for light, crisp results.

Rolling out

Dust a cool surface and your rolling pin lightly with flour. Roll lightly and evenly in one direction, always away from you, moving the pastry around by a quarter turn occasionally. Try to keep the pastry even in shape and thickness. Avoid stretching the pastry, which will cause it to shrink during cooking. Depending on the recipe, shortcrust pastry is usually rolled to about 3 mm (⅛ inch) thick; puff pastry can be rolled slightly thicker, to about 5 mm (¼ inch).

Lining a tart tin

Put the flan ring or tart tin on a baking sheet. Roll out the pastry to about 5 cm (2 inches) larger all around than the diameter of the tin. Roll the pastry loosely around the rolling pin, lift it over the tin, then carefully unroll it into the tin. Gently ease the pastry into the tin, pressing it into the flutes with your finger and taking care not to stretch it or leave air gaps. Turn any surplus pastry outwards from the rim and then roll the rolling pin over the top so that the surplus pastry is cut and falls away.

HOW MUCH PASTRY?

When a recipe gives a guide to the quantity of shortcrust pastry required, the weight refers to the amount of flour. For example, if the recipe requires 200 g (7 oz) shortcrust pastry or pâte brisée, make the dough from 200 g (7 oz) flour, plus fat and other ingredients in proportion. Here is a rough guide to how much pastry you will need for different sizes of tart tin:

Tart tin diameter	Quantity of pastry
18 cm (7 inch)	125 g (4 oz)
20 cm (8 inch)	175 g (6 oz)
23 cm (9 inch)	200 g (7 oz)
25 cm (10 inch)	250 g (8 oz)

Baking blind

This is the process of part-baking pastry in the tin before the filling is added to ensure crisp results. The pastry is weighted down to prevent it from bubbling up or falling down around the sides. Line the tart tin with the rolled-out dough as usual and prick the base of the pastry with a fork, so that any air trapped underneath can escape rather than cause the pastry to bubble up and form an uneven surface.

Place a square of nonstick baking paper in the pastry case and, taking care not to damage the edges of the pastry, half-fill the paper with dried beans or ceramic baking beans. Bake as instructed in the recipe, usually for 10–15 minutes, then remove the paper and beans. Return the pastry case to the oven for about 5 minutes to crisp the base if necessary. You can use crumpled foil instead of beans if you prefer.

Using filo pastry

Filo pastry has a reputation for being difficult to handle, but if you follow these simple guidelines, you will find that it is no more difficult to use than any other pastry. To keep filo soft and workable, make sure the pastry is covered all the time you are not actually working on it. Lay a sheet of clingfilm or a damp tea towel over it or keep it wrapped, because it will

become brittle and break easily if it dries out. Have your other ingredients or fillings, together with a pastry brush, close to hand so that you can complete the recipe before the sheets dry out.

Work quickly, out of direct sunlight, using up any broken or torn pieces of filo between whole sheets – no one will notice. Do not moisten with water, which makes the sheets stick together and disintegrate, and keep the work surface dry for the same reason. Use fat, such as melted butter, and a pastry brush to seal edges and to brush the pastry for crisp results. Filo pastry can be baked or fried.

Storing pastry

Pastry is best frozen ready shaped, whether cooked or uncooked. Freeze cases or pies in foil containers or freezerproof dishes. Empty pastry cases can be cooked from frozen; add an extra 5 minutes to the conventional cooking time. Filled pies are best defrosted before they are baked to ensure they are cooked through evenly. Pastry can be stored in the freezer for up to three months.

Rubbed-in pastry mix can be stored in the refrigerator for up to seven days. Alternatively, it may be frozen for three months. Allow to thaw completely before adding the water.

Pastry decorations

A modest decoration is part of the traditional look of pies and tarts. Leaves, a lattice and fancy edges all enhance the appeal and are very simple to make.

Flaking or knocking up

It's important to seal pastry neatly to prevent fillings from leaking out. Hold one finger lightly against the top of the pastry rim and press the blade of a knife horizontally into the cut pastry edge, making a series of shallow cuts. Do this all around the edge.

Plait

Cut three long, narrow strips of pastry. Pinch them together at one end and press on to the rim of the pie. Plait the strips around the pie, joining in extra lengths of pastry as necessary. Tuck the ends under.

Twist

Cut two long, thin strips of pastry and pinch them together at one end. Attach to the pie rim and then twist the strips gently, arranging them around the pie edge as you go.

Scallops

This decorative finish adds a professional touch and helps to seal the edge firmly. Place the knife blade at a vertical angle against the pastry edge and press your fingertip next to it on the rim. Make a vertical cut, pulling slightly upwards, to create a scallop. Continue around the edge at intervals of about 1.5 cm (¾ inch).

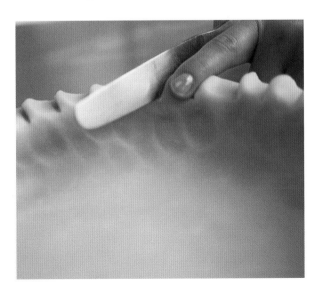

Crimping

This is a quick alternative to flaking and scalloping. Push the finger of one hand into the top of the pastry rim. At the same time, pinch the outer edge with the finger and thumb of the other hand, pinching the pastry to a point. Continue crimping all around the edge.

Leaves

A decorative border of pastry leaves works well on a tart with a smooth, plain filling. Pile any pastry trimmings on top of each other in a stack – do not press them into a ball because they will rise unevenly. Roll the pastry out to about 3 mm (⅛ inch) thick.

Cut the pastry into long, narrow strips, about 2.5 cm (1 inch) wide. Make diagonal cuts across the strips to create diamonds. Press a knife against the pastry to mark the veins. Arrange the leaves so that they overlap on top of the pie, securing them by brushing them underneath with a little water, milk or beaten egg.

Lattice

Keep the lattice strips apart, leaving wide gaps to show the filling or arrange them almost touching to make a closed lattice top. Cut the pastry into long, narrow strips. Starting at one side, overlap the strips, weaving them under and over each other, to make a wide trellis. Attach to the edge by moistening with a little water and pressing in place. Trim the excess.

Basic pastry recipes

Good pastry takes practice, but do persevere as the results are very impressive. To make a delicate pastry, always handle the dough lightly and allow it enough time to rest between each handling.

Shortcrust pastry

The classic choice for everyday savoury and sweet dishes, shortcrust pastry is easy to handle and holds its shape well for pies and tart cases.

Preparation time about 10 minutes, plus chilling
Makes 200 g (7 oz)

200 g (7 oz) plain flour
pinch of salt
100 g (3½ oz) fat, such as equal quantities of butter and white vegetable fat
2–3 tablespoons iced water

❶ Sift the flour and salt into a bowl. Cut the fat into small pieces and add it to the flour.

❷ Use your fingertips to rub the fat into the flour very lightly and evenly until it begins to resemble fine breadcrumbs.

❸ Sprinkle the water over the surface and stir with a palette knife until the mixture begins to clump together.

❹ Turn out the pastry on to a lightly floured surface and press it together lightly with your fingers. Cover and chill for about 30 minutes before use.

Pâte sucrée

A sweet, enriched shortcrust pastry, this has a rich, biscuit-like texture suitable for sweet tarts and pastries. This recipe makes enough pastry to line a 20 cm (8 inch) tart tin.

Preparation time about 10 minutes, plus chilling
Makes 175 g (6 oz)

175 g (6 oz) plain flour
pinch of salt
75 g (3 oz) unsalted butter, slightly softened
2 egg yolks
1 tablespoon cold water
40 g (1½ oz) caster sugar

1 Sift the flour and salt into a pile on a cold work surface and make a well in the centre. Add the butter, egg yolks, water and sugar to the well.

2 Use the fingertips of one hand to work the ingredients together into a rough paste. The mixture should resemble scrambled eggs. Gradually work in the flour with your fingertips to bind the mixture into a smooth dough. Press together lightly and form into a ball.

3 Wrap in clingfilm and chill for about 30 minutes before use.

Puff pastry

Well-made puff pastry will rise to about six times its height when it is cooked. Although it has a reputation for being difficult to make, the most important guideline is to keep all the ingredients cool.

Preparation time about 30 minutes, plus chilling
Makes 250 g (8 oz)

250 g (8 oz) plain flour
pinch of salt
250 g (8 oz) cooled butter in one piece
1 teaspoon lemon juice
150 ml (¼ pint) iced water

1 Sift the flour and salt into a bowl. Rub in a quarter of the butter until it resembles breadcrumbs. Add the lemon juice and most of the water. Mix to a dough and gradually add the rest of the water to form a dry dough. On a lightly floured surface knead the dough into a ball and flatten. Wrap it in clingfilm and chill for about 30 minutes. Put the rest of the butter between two sheets of clingfilm and roll it out to a square 1 cm (½ inch) thick. Unwrap the chilled pastry and roll it out to form a square large enough to wrap round the butter. Put the butter in the centre of the pastry square. Fold over the edges to encase the butter.

2 Lightly dust the work surface and roll out the pastry to a rectangle about 1 cm (½ inch) thick. Fold the bottom third on to the middle third, then fold the top third over the top. Wrap and chill for 15 minutes.

3 Return the pastry to the work surface with a short edge facing towards you. Press down on the edges then roll it out into a rectangle and fold as before. Repeat 6 times then chill. Roll out to its final shape then chill again for 30 minutes. Knock up the edges (see page 45) so that the layers rise properly.

Choux pastry

This breaks all the rules for pastry making: choux needs lots of heat and firm handling for good results. Use it for sweet or savoury buns, profiteroles, beignets and éclairs.

Preparation time about 10 minutes
Makes 75 g (3 oz)

75 g (3 oz) plain flour
pinch of salt
50 g (2 oz) unsalted butter
150 ml (¼ pint) water or equal quantities of water and milk
2 large eggs, lightly beaten

❶ Sift the flour and salt together on to a sheet of greaseproof paper. Place the butter and water in a saucepan and heat gently until the butter melts, then bring to the boil. Do not bring to the boil before the butter has melted.

❷ Draw the pan off the heat and immediately add the flour, all at once. Beat with a wooden spoon or electric hand mixer until the mixture forms a smooth ball that leaves the sides of the pan clean. Do not overbeat at this stage or the paste will become oily.

❸ Leave the mixture to cool for 2 minutes. Gradually add the eggs, beating hard after each addition, and continue to beat until the mixture is smooth and glossy. The paste should be just soft enough to fall gently from the spoon. Use the pastry immediately or cover closely and chill until needed.

Cakes

A piece of cake, accompanied by a cup of coffee or tea, is everyone's favourite comfort food. Sweet and indulgent, it fills that little gap between meals, and as a treat it's raised to new heights when the cake is freshly homemade.

Lining cake tins
Use greaseproof paper (or non-stick baking paper) and brush the tin's interior base and sides with melted butter before you start lining. Most cakes need a completely lined tin but some need only the base lined.

Round tins
Using the tin as a guide, draw a circle on greaseproof paper and cut it out. Cut strips of paper a little wider than the height of the tin, fold over a lip approximately 1 cm (½ inch) wide and snip it at intervals. Brush the sides and base with melted butter and fit the paper around the sides of the tin so that the lip sits flat on the base. Press the circle of paper into the base and brush all the paper with more melted butter.

Sandwich tins
Cut out circles of greaseproof paper, using the tins as a guide. Grease the tins and line their bases with the paper circles. Alternatively, grease the tins, tip in a little flour and tilt each tin to coat the base and sides.

Square tins
Use the same technique as for round tins, but once you've cut the square base and strips, make snips only where the paper fits the corners of the tin.

Loaf tins
A long strip of paper that covers the base and long sides is usually enough lining for a loaf tin, and this arrangement makes lifting the cake out easy. If the tin needs lining fully, add two further strips of paper at the short ends.

Shallow rectangular and Swiss roll tins
Cut a rectangle of greaseproof paper that is 8 cm (3 inches) longer and wider than the cake tin. Press the paper into the greased tin, snipping it at the corners so that it fits neatly.

Ring tins
Brush the ring tin thoroughly with melted butter. Tip a little flour into the base of the tin and tilt it until the base and sides are evenly coated with flour. Tap out the excess flour.

Paper cake liners
These tin liners are like giant paper muffin cases and can be bought to slip into loaf tins and round cake tins. Although they are not readily available in many sizes, they are easy to use and particularly convenient if you need to transport your cakes to parties. When removed, the liners leave ridged indentations around the cake.

Cake-making methods

There are several basic techniques used in cake making. Being aware of the different processes will help you achieve good results every time.

Creamed cakes

Creaming is the traditional method of making sandwich cakes and buttery sponges. The butter must be very soft so that it has a smooth, creamy consistency when it is beaten with the sugar. When it is thoroughly creamed the mixture should be much paler in colour than the butter alone was, and it should also be very soft. This stage is often described as being 'light and fluffy'.

The beaten eggs are added a little at a time. If the eggs are added too quickly the mixture will curdle, which might affect the texture of the cake. If this happens, add a little of the flour, before finally stirring in the rest of the flour with a metal spoon.

Whisked cakes

The whisking method is used to make an aerated, fatless sponge. It's the air that's trapped in the mixture that gives a whisked cake volume. A whisked mixture is more delicate than a creamed mixture, so take care throughout to keep it aerated and light. Standing the bowl over a pan of simmering water helps to speed up

whisking. Plain flour is folded in to stabilize the mixture, and it's important to do this as gently as possible so that the foamy consistency is not lost.

Melted cakes

This quick and easy method is used for cakes such as gingerbread, in which the butter and sugars are melted together before being mixed with the dry ingredients. These cakes have a dense but moist texture and rely on baking powder and bicarbonate of soda to make them rise. It's important to bake the cake as soon as the ingredients are mixed together because the raising agents are activated when the wet and dry ingredients are combined. Melted cakes keep well and often improve in flavour and texture if they are wrapped and stored for a couple of days before being eaten.

Rubbed-in cakes

Used for muffins, crumble cakes and rock buns, this method resembles the one used for homemade pastry. The butter is rubbed into the flour with the fingertips or, more conveniently, in a food processor, before the remaining ingredients are added. With the exception of crumble cakes, rubbed-in cakes contain a small proportion of butter and usually go stale quite quickly. They are generally best eaten on the day they are made.

Basic techniques

Here are some of the standard techniques that crop up repeatedly in cake recipes.

Softening butter

All cakes made using the creamed method require softened butter. This is most easily done in the microwave, because few of us will remember to remove the butter from the refrigerator well in advance. Soften it in a few short bursts. The butter should be soft enough that you can push into it with your finger.

Melting chocolate

See page 56 for instructions on melting chocolate. If you are melting chocolate with other ingredients – butter, milk or cream, for example – watch closely as the high fat content will speed up the melting.

Folding in

Flours, flavourings, melted butter or whisked egg whites are usually 'folded' gently into creamed cake and sponge mixes rather than beaten in. The aim is to keep the mixture light and aerated. Push a large metal spoon down into the mixture and lift it up and over the ingredients you've added so that you start folding them together. Keep mixing together in this way, using a very gentle action and turning the bowl slowly with your other hand until the ingredients are just blended.

When you are adding whisked egg whites to a mixture, fold in about a quarter of the quantity before adding the remainder. The first batch will be useful in lightening the mixture, particularly if it's very firm, which will make it easier for you to fold in the rest of the eggs.

Levelling

Once a cake mixture has been turned into the baking tin, it needs to be levelled. This is so that firm mixtures – like fruit cakes and sponges – cook evenly and do not emerge from the oven looking lopsided, and so that whisked sponges are spread to fill the whole tin. Use the back of a large metal spoon to spread the mixture in an even layer. Spread whisked sponges gently into

the corners of square tins so you don't deflate all the air you've incorporated. Loose sponges, batters and melted mixtures will usually find their own level.

Checking that a cake is cooked

Try not to be impatient when you are waiting for a cake to cook. Repeatedly opening the oven door, allowing a rush of cold air into the oven, might cause the cake to sink in the middle. Check that a cake is cooked shortly before it's due to come out of the oven. If it's slightly domed in the centre, has a baked colour and doesn't 'give' in the centre when lightly touched with a flat hand, it's ready. Fruit cakes and other deep cakes can be checked further by pushing a fine skewer into the centre: the skewer should come out just clean. If there's still raw mixture clinging to the skewer, pop the cake back in the oven for a little longer.

Exceptions are really moist chocolate cakes and brownies. Brownies should feel very loose under the crust because of the high sugar content.

Cooling cakes on a wire rack

Most sponge cakes should be removed carefully from the tin as soon as you've taken them out of the oven. Loosening the edges of the cake with a knife will help you to release it if you haven't lined the sides. Rich fruit cakes, however, should be left in the tin until they have cooled completely.

Whipping cream until peaking

To sandwich or cover sponge cakes use double or whipping cream (or half cream and half crème fraîche or mascarpone) and whisk in a bowl with any additional flavours, such as liqueur, flavour extracts or sugar. Use a hand-held electric whisk or a balloon whisk and beat, vigorously at first and then more slowly as it starts to thicken. The aim is to get the cream to form peaks that only just hold their shape, bearing in mind that the cream will continue to thicken as you spread it over the cake.

Storing cakes

A light, buttery sponge cake definitely tastes at its best – even if it is a little difficult to slice – on the day it is made, but it won't spoil if it's stored for several days. Other cakes, such as gingerbread, might actually improve in flavour and texture if they are stored for a few days before eating, and rich fruit cakes mature in flavour when stored for a month or more. If you are storing a cake for any length of time, keep the lining paper in place because this will help prevent the cake from drying out. Store in an airtight container or wrapped in foil, in a cool place. Avoid putting cakes in the refrigerator, unless hot weather means you've no other way of storing a cake decorated with fresh cream or cream cheese frosting. Light sponge cakes and Madeira cakes also freeze well.

Yeasted cakes

Sweet yeasted cakes are made in a similar way to basic breads, but they take a long time to prove because of the richness of the dough. To accelerate the process the yeast should first be mixed with a little warm liquid and a dash of sugar, leaving it for 10 minutes or until frothy. This starts the yeast working and is an indication of whether the yeast is fresh – if it doesn't turn frothy, don't continue until you've bought more yeast.

Kneading yeasted cakes by hand on your work surface will take about 10 minutes. Alternatively, you can use a machine – a table-top electric whisk with a dough hook attachment is ideal. This will take

4–5 minutes and allow you to get on with other things. Check the consistency of the dough during kneading. It should feel soft but not so sticky that it clings to your hands or around the sides of the mixer. If necessary, sprinkle the mixture with a little more flour.

Yeasted cakes are left to prove (rise) twice, once in the mixing bowl and again when shaped. The first proving can be accelerated slightly in the microwave. Use full power for 15 seconds (but no longer or the dough might start to cook) and leave for 15 minutes. Repeat two or three times.

Knocking back

Once the dough has risen until it has doubled in size it must be knocked back to deflate the air. Do this by simply punching the dough with a clenched fist, so that it's ready to shape or roll before the second proving. If you find when rolling the dough that it keeps shrinking back to its original size, cover it with a cloth and leave it for 10 minutes. You will then find it much easier to work with.

Checking that a cake is cooked

To tell whether a yeasted cake is cooked through tap it gently on the base, if necessary removing it from its tin first. It should sound hollow. If not, return it to the oven. Yeasted cakes taste best when freshly baked and still slightly warm. They also freeze well for another day, in which case warm them through before serving.

Basic cake toppings

A plain sponge cake can be lifted to another dimension with an indulgent topping. A classic buttercream perfectly complements most cakes, and can be flavoured for added interest. Glacé icing looks great drizzled over gingerbread.

Buttercream

The best buttercream is very soft and fluffy, with a flavour that's not too overpoweringly sweet. Make a coffee-flavoured alternative by dissolving 1 tablespoon instant espresso powder in 2 teaspoons boiling water and beating it into the buttercream.

Preparation time 3 minutes
Makes enough to sandwich and spread over the top of an 18–20 cm (7–8 inch) cake or to cover the top and sides

100 g (3½ oz) unsalted butter, softened
150 g (5 oz) icing sugar

1 Beat the butter in a bowl with a little of the sugar until smooth.

2 Add the remaining sugar and beat until pale and fluffy. Add a few drops of boiling water and beat for a few moments more.

Glacé icing

Using lemon or lime juice instead of water in glacé icing gives a welcome tang that helps balance the sweetness of the sugar. Most icing sugars are free flowing, rather than caking together in lumps in the packet, but if you open a pack that's a bit lumpy, sift it first.

Preparation time 2 minutes
Makes enough to cover thinly the top of an 18–20 cm (7–8 inch) cake

75 g (3 oz) icing sugar
2 teaspoons lemon or lime juice

1 Put the icing sugar in a bowl, sifting it first if it's at all lumpy.

2 Add the juice and beat until smooth. Spread over the warm or cooled cake (depending on the recipe).

Cream cheese frosting

This is a lovely tangy frosting with plenty of flavour, and it's great for anyone who doesn't like intensely sugary spreads. Taste for sweetness once it's whisked – you can easily beat in another 25 g (1 oz) sugar if it's not sweet enough. If you prefer, use mascarpone cheese instead of cream cheese and chill it in the refrigerator for an hour if it's too soft to spread.

Preparation time 3 minutes
Makes enough to sandwich and spread over the top of an 18–20 cm (7–8 inch) cake or to cover the top and sides

200 g (7 oz) full-fat cream cheese
1–2 teaspoons lime or lemon juice
75 g (3 oz) icing sugar

1. Beat the cream cheese in a bowl until it is softened and smooth. Beat in 1 teaspoon juice.

2. Add the icing sugar and beat until smooth, adding a little more juice if the mixture is very firm.

Coconut frosting

This seriously rich icing is perfect for spreading over the angel cake on page 236, but it's also great for adding a lively flavour to a plain Victoria sandwich, in which case you could match the frosting's tropical theme by sandwiching the cake with a tropical fruit jam.

Preparation time 5 minutes
Cooking time 2–3 minutes
Makes enough to cover the top of an 18–20 cm (7–8 inch) cake

75 ml (3 fl oz) single cream
50 g (2 oz) creamed coconut, chopped
2–3 teaspoons lemon or lime juice
300 g (10 oz) icing sugar

1. Put the cream and creamed coconut in a small saucepan and heat gently until melted.

2. Turn into a bowl and whisk in the lemon or lime juice and icing sugar until it is fairly thick and smooth.

Chocolate

Whether it is comfortingly baked in a rich pudding, lavishly swirled into a creamy dessert or simply snapped from a bar, chocolate is one of our favourite foods. Have fun experimenting with chocolate's incredible versatility.

Types of chocolate

When you buy plain or milk chocolate, remember that the higher the proportion of cocoa solids, the purer the chocolate flavour will be. The darkest plain chocolate contains 80 per cent or more cocoa solids and has an intensely chocolatey flavour. Slightly sweeter is plain chocolate that contains 60–70 per cent cocoa solids. This has a dense chocolatey flavour and is a good 'all-rounder'. It melts well to a smooth, glossy texture and retains its full flavour.

Milk chocolate is considerably sweeter than plain and has added milk, sugar and flavourings, such as vanilla. It contains 20–30 per cent cocoa solids. White chocolate contains no solids. Instead, it is made with cocoa butter and milk, sugar and flavouring.

Cocoa powder, a by-product of the processing method, has a strong, bitter flavour. Good for intensifying the flavour of chocolate, it should always be cooked and needs additional sweetening.

Never use chocolate-flavoured cake covering. It's an imitation chocolate-flavoured bar of sugar, vegetable oils and flavourings.

Melting chocolate

On the hob

Break the chocolate into pieces and place them in a heatproof bowl. Rest the bowl over a pan of gently simmering water, making sure that the base of the bowl doesn't touch the water. Once the chocolate starts to melt, turn off the heat and leave it until it is completely melted, stirring once or twice until smooth. It's crucial that no water gets into the bowl while the chocolate is melting – steam, for example – because this will make the melted chocolate solidify. When you are pouring the melted chocolate on to paper for making chocolate decorations, wipe the base of the bowl with a cloth as soon as you take it from the heat so that no condensed steam drips into the chocolate.

In the microwave

Use a microwave-proof bowl and melt the broken chocolate pieces on medium power in one-minute spurts, checking frequently.

In the oven

Put the chocolate in a small ovenproof bowl or dish and leave the bowl in a low oven, 110°C (225°F), Gas Mark ¼, checking frequently. Alternatively, put it in an oven that's been switched off after baking.

Using chocolate

Chocolate can be grated, curled, scribbled or melted and modelled. Some techniques take a matter of minutes, while other more sculptural forms require a little more patience and planning. Chocolate decorations keep in a cool place for up to a week.

Grated chocolate

Scatter coarsely grated plain, milk or white chocolate over creamy desserts, ice creams and chilled drinks to make them look really appealing. If the chocolate bar is difficult to grate and breaks into tiny, brittle specks, warm it, very briefly, in the microwave first.

Chocolate scribbles

Line a tray with nonstick baking paper. Fill a paper piping bag with a little melted chocolate and snip off the merest tip. 'Draw' shapes on the paper – scribbled

lines, curvy swirls or filigree patterns – and leave to set. Peel the paper away from the scribbles and use them to decorate chilled desserts. Don't make the patterns too delicate or they will break.

Chocolate curls

Use a potato peeler to pare off thick curls of chocolate from a bar and scatter them over cheesecakes, ice cream, trifles, cakes and chocolate mousses. The chunkier the chocolate bar, the larger the curls will be. Again, soften the bar, very briefly, in the microwave before use if it's too brittle.

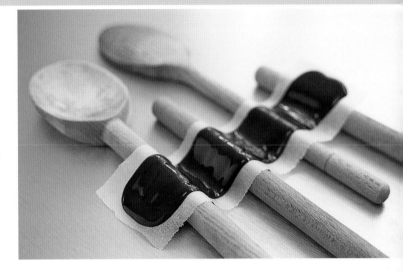

Chocolate caraque

These professional-looking curls take a little more effort but are well worth making for a special cake or dessert. They'll keep well in the refrigerator for several weeks or in the freezer for longer. Spread melted chocolate in a thin layer on a marble slab or a clean, smooth surface, such as a new, plastic chopping board or sturdy baking sheet. Leave to set. Holding a knife at an angle, draw it across the chocolate so that you scrape off curls. If the chocolate is too soft and doesn't curl, pop it in the refrigerator for a few minutes. If it is brittle and breaks off in thin shards, leave it at room temperature for a while before trying again.

Chocolate shavings

To make more elaborate curls for special cakes and desserts gently melt 300 g (10 oz) plain or white chocolate with 25 g (1 oz) unsalted butter. Turn the mixture into a clean and dry 250 g (8 oz) butter or margarine tub and leave until set but not brittle. Remove from the tub and pare off shavings. Protect the end of the slab with foil so that the heat of your hand does not melt the chocolate.

Chocolate leaves

Firm but flexible leaves, such as fresh bay or rose, are best for making decorations for festive desserts and chocolate logs. Thoroughly wash and dry the leaves and brush or spoon a little chocolate on to the underside. Leave to set then gently peel away the leaf.

Chocolate ribbons

Cut out 15 x 3 cm (6 x 1¼ inch) strips of nonstick baking paper. Spread melted chocolate over the strips, almost to the edges. Arrange six small wooden spoons, pens or chunky pencils in a row and spaced slightly apart. Lift the chocolate strips over them so that they set in ribbony waves. When set carefully peel away the paper.

Jagged chocolate brittle

Spread melted chocolate on a tray or baking sheet lined with nonstick baking paper. If you like, scatter some finely chopped toasted nuts over the chocolate, chill until really brittle, then peel away the paper and snap the chocolate into jagged shards. Spear into chocolate desserts and special-occasion cakes.

Cut-outs

Use small biscuit or cake cutters (available from specialist shops) to make shapes for decorating cakes and desserts. Spread melted chocolate on a tray lined with nonstick baking paper. Leave it to set then press out the shapes with the cutters.

Chocolate-dipped morsels

This is a great serving idea for summer fruits, such as strawberries and cherries, or for covering chocolate fudge, truffles or nuts. Half-dip the fruit into melted chocolate, let the excess drip off and place the fruit on a sheet of nonstick baking paper until set.

Basic chocolate recipes

Almost everyone loves a good chocolate sauce, the darker and glossier the better. Serve it with hot chocolate puddings or spooned generously over vanilla ice cream. For topping cakes, you can't beat a rich ganache.

  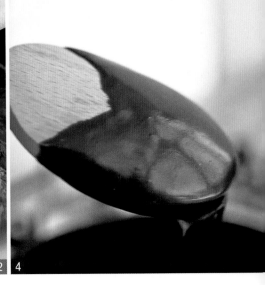

Glossy chocolate sauce

This sauce is perfect with ice cream, fruit or puddings. If it is made in advance chocolate sauce will solidify, so reheat it very gently so that the chocolate doesn't spoil.

Preparation time 5 minutes
Cooking time 3 minutes
Serves 6

125 g (4 oz) caster sugar
200 g (7 oz) plain chocolate, chopped
25 g (1 oz) unsalted butter

1 Put the sugar in a small heavy-based saucepan with 125 ml (4 fl oz) water. Cook over a low heat, stirring constantly with a wooden spoon, until the sugar has completely dissolved.

2 Bring to the boil and boil for 1 minute, then leave to cool for a further minute. Add the chocolate and butter and leave until both have melted.

3 Stir until smooth and glossy, returning to a gentle heat if the last of the chocolate doesn't melt completely.

4 The chocolate sauce is the correct consistency when it is smooth and glossy, and coats the back of a wooden spoon.

Rich chocolate ganache

Chocolate ganache sounds rather exotic, but it is simply a blend of chocolate and cream, which is easy to make and one of the most useful components of chocolate baking. Use it as a cake filling or topping or as a basic mixture for chocolate truffles.

Preparation time 5 minutes, plus cooling
Cooking time 3 minutes
Makes sufficient to cover a 20 cm (8 inch) chocolate cake

300 ml (½ pint) double cream
300 g (10 oz) plain chocolate, chopped

1 Heat the cream in a medium-sized, heavy-based saucepan until it is bubbling around the edges. Remove from the heat and add the chocolate.

2 Leave to stand for a few minutes until the chocolate has melted, then stir well and turn the mixture into a bowl.

3 Chill for 15–45 minutes or until the mixture holds its shape when stirred.

White chocolate ganache

White chocolate is more temperamental to cook with than plain, so the technique for making ganache is slightly different. Once made, use it in exactly the same way.

Preparation time 5 minutes, plus chilling
Cooking time 3 minutes
Makes sufficient to cover a 20 cm (8 inch) chocolate cake

300 ml (½ pint) double cream
300 g (10 oz) white chocolate, chopped

1 Put half the cream in a medium-sized, heavy-based saucepan and heat gently until it is bubbling around the edges. Remove from the heat and stir in the chopped chocolate.

2 Leave to stand for a few minutes or until the chocolate has melted, then stir lightly and turn into a bowl. Chill for about 15 minutes until cool.

3 Add the remaining cream to the bowl and whisk with a hand-held electric mixer until the ganache just starts to hold its shape. Don't over-whisk or it will start to separate.

STARTERS

Red pepper soup with goats' cheese croutons

For best results, use 'pointed' red peppers, which are sweet and have a fuller flavour than the round ones. Gently sautéing the peppers and onion in the oil will also intensify the flavour of the soup.

Preparation time 15 minutes

Cooking time 45 minutes

Serves 6

4 tablespoons olive oil, plus extra to drizzle

2 red onions, sliced

5 red peppers, deseeded and roughly chopped

2 teaspoons caster sugar

2 garlic cloves, chopped

2 tablespoons chopped oregano, plus extra to garnish

900 ml (1½ pints) Chicken or Vegetable Stock (see pages 18–19)

400 g (13 oz) can chopped tomatoes

2 tablespoons sun-dried tomato paste

6 thin slices baguette

150 g (5 oz) goats' cheese, cut into 6 slices

salt and pepper

1 Heat 4 tablespoons oil in a large saucepan. Add the onions and red peppers and cook gently, stirring frequently, for 10 minutes. Add the sugar, garlic and oregano and fry for a further 5–10 minutes or until the peppers are soft.

2 Add the stock, tomatoes, tomato paste and a little seasoning and bring to the boil. Reduce the heat and simmer gently for 20 minutes.

3 Use a stick blender to blend the soup until pulpy. Alternatively, blend in batches in a food processor.

4 Toast the bread on one side. Turn over the slices and top with the slices of cheese. Grill for a further 2–3 minutes until the cheese is beginning to colour.

5 Reheat the soup and ladle it into individual warm bowls. Add a toasted cheese slice to each, drizzle with a little oil and serve scattered with oregano.

Creamy pumpkin soup with harissa

This smooth and creamy soup is zipped up with harissa sauce, which is stirred in at the table to add a spicy edge. Serve the extra sauce in a bowl for those who like a hotter flavour.

Preparation time 25 minutes
Cooking time 35 minutes
Serves 6

1 kg (2 lb) pumpkin
4 tablespoons olive oil
2 onions, chopped
2 garlic cloves, crushed
1 litre (1¾ pints) Vegetable Stock (see page 19)
100 ml (3½ fl oz) double cream
salt and pepper
chopped coriander, to garnish
1 quantity Hot Harissa Sauce (see page 130), to serve

1 Scoop out the seeds and cut away the skin from the pumpkin. Chop the flesh into chunks. Heat the oil in a large, heavy-based saucepan and gently fry the onions for 5 minutes. Add the garlic and fry for a further 1 minute.

2 Add the pumpkin and stock and bring to the boil. Reduce the heat, cover with a lid and cook gently for 20–25 minutes or until the pumpkin is soft and mushy.

3 Use a stick blender to blend the soup until pulpy. Alternatively, blend in batches in a food processor.

4 Return to the saucepan, stir in half the cream and season to taste. Reheat gently.

5 Ladle into individual warm soup bowls and spoon a little of the harissa sauce over each. Serve drizzled with the remaining cream.

Beef and noodle broth

This easy soup relies on good-quality, well-flavoured stock and is ideal for using up any leftover beef or chicken stock. Slice the beef across the grain, so that it falls into tender, succulent strips.

Preparation time 15 minutes
Cooking time 10 minutes
Serves 2

300 g (10 oz) rump or sirloin steak
15 g (½ oz) fresh root ginger, grated
2 teaspoons soy sauce
50 g (2 oz) vermicelli rice noodles
600 ml (1 pint) Beef or Chicken Stock (see page 18)
1 red chilli, deseeded and finely chopped
1 garlic clove, thinly sliced
2 teaspoons caster sugar
2 teaspoons vegetable oil
75 g (3 oz) sugar snap peas, halved lengthways
small handful of Thai basil, torn into pieces

❶ Trim any fat from the beef. Mix the ginger with 1 teaspoon soy sauce and smooth the mixture over both sides of the beef. Cook the noodles according to the directions on the packet. Drain and rinse thoroughly in cold water.

❷ Put the stock in a large, heavy-based saucepan and bring it to a gentle simmer with the chilli, garlic and sugar. Cover and cook gently for 5 minutes.

❸ Meanwhile, heat the oil in a small, heavy-based frying pan and fry the beef for 2 minutes on each side. Transfer the meat to a board, cut it in half lengthways and then cut it across into thin strips.

❹ Add the noodles, peas, basil and remaining soy sauce to the soup and heat gently for 1 minute. Stir in the beef and serve immediately.

Minestrone

There are many regional variations on minestrone, and this recipe combines elements of them all. You can use all sorts of vegetable odds and ends. It also reheats well the next day.

Preparation time 20 minutes

Cooking time 1½ hours

Serves 6

2 tablespoons olive oil, plus extra for drizzling

1 onion, chopped

3 carrots, chopped

3 celery sticks, chopped

2 garlic cloves, thinly sliced

400 g (13 oz) can cannellini beans, drained and rinsed

400 g (13 oz) can plum tomatoes or 6 fresh tomatoes, skinned (see page 17) and chopped

150 g (5 oz) peas or broad beans

1 large potato, diced

2 courgettes, diced

1.5 litres (2½ pints) Chicken or Vegetable Stock (see pages 18–19)

150 g (5 oz) cavolo nero or spinach

75 g (3 oz) small dried pasta shapes

salt and pepper

To serve

grated Parmesan or pecorino cheese

homemade or bought pesto

1. Heat the oil in a large, heavy-based saucepan and gently fry the onion, carrots and celery for 5 minutes. Add the garlic and fry for a further 2 minutes.

2. Add the beans, tomatoes, peas or beans, potato, courgettes and stock to the pan and bring gently to a simmer. Cover and simmer gently for about 1 hour or until all the vegetables are tender.

3. Shred the cavolo nero or spinach into thin strips and add to the pan.

4. Add the pasta and stir gently. Cover and cook for 10 minutes or until the pasta is cooked. Season. Ladle into individual warm, shallow bowls, drizzle with extra olive oil and serve with the grated Parmesan or pecorino and pesto.

Clam chowder

A kilo of clams provides surprisingly little meat, but the pronounced flavour, combined with the salt pork, makes a rich, hearty soup that's good as a starter or, in larger portions, as a main course.

Preparation time 20 minutes
Cooking time 30 minutes
Serves 4

1 kg (2 lb) clams, cleaned (see page 39)
200 g (7 oz) salt pork, finely chopped
1 large onion, chopped
15 g (½ oz) butter
1 tablespoon plain flour
4 tomatoes, skinned (see page 17) and chopped
350 g (11½ oz) potatoes, diced
2 bay leaves
3 tablespoons chopped parsley
2 teaspoons Tabasco sauce
150 ml (¼ pint) single cream

❶ Bring 150 ml (¼ pint) water to the boil in a saucepan. Add the clams, cover with a tight-fitting lid and cook for 4–5 minutes or until the shells have opened. Drain, reserving the cooking juices, and discard any that remain closed. Remove the flesh from the shells and chop it into small pieces.

❷ Put the pork and onion in a large saucepan with a knob of the butter and fry gently for 10 minutes or until browned. Stir in the remaining butter until melted. Add the flour and cook, stirring, for 1 minute.

❸ Add the clam cooking juices and 450 ml (¾ pint) water, the tomatoes, potatoes and bay leaves. Bring just to the boil, then reduce the heat, cover and cook very gently for 15 minutes or until the potatoes are tender.

❹ Stir in the clams and parsley and cook very gently for a further 2 minutes. Add the Tabasco sauce and cream, heat through and serve.

Potted prawns with fennel pittas

Submerged in mildly spiced, garlicky butter, these little pots of freshly cooked prawns are a fabulous 'make-ahead' starter.

Preparation time 20 minutes, plus chilling
Cooking time 15 minutes
Serves 4

200 g (7 oz) butter
1 small head of fennel, finely chopped
1 teaspoon finely grated lemon rind
1 teaspoon fennel seeds, crushed
4 small round pitta breads
350 g (11½ oz) raw peeled prawns
1 garlic clove, crushed
good pinch of paprika
¼ teaspoon ground mace
salt and pepper

❶ Melt 15 g (½ oz) butter in a frying pan and fry the fennel gently for about 5 minutes or until soft. Stir in the lemon rind, fennel seeds and seasoning. Split the pittas down one side and spread the fennel mixture inside. Flatten them firmly under your palms.

❷ Melt another 25 g (1 oz) butter in a large frying pan and gently fry the prawns for about 2 minutes, turning once, or until they are deep pink on both sides. (Fry them in batches if necessary.) Return all the prawns to the pan and stir in the garlic, paprika and mace.

❸ Pack the prawns into 4 individual ramekin dishes, each holding 125 ml (4 fl oz). Melt the remaining butter in a small saucepan, skimming off any foam from the surface. Spoon over the prawns so that they are mostly submerged. Cover and chill for 2 hours or until the butter has set.

❹ Heat a ridged grill pan or grill and lightly toast the pittas on both sides. Cut into fingers and serve with the prawns.

Scallops with asparagus and frazzled bacon

Sautéeing scallops in bacon juices and serving with asparagus is such a simple treat for this very special shellfish.

Preparation time 15 minutes
Cooking time 25 minutes
Serves 4

½ small leek
300 g (10 oz) asparagus
50 η (2 oz) butter
2 tablespoons single cream
75 g (3 oz) thin-cut rashers of smoked streaky bacon
12 plump shelled scallops (see page 39)
salt and pepper
4 tablespoons chopped chervil or parsley, to serve

❶ Trim and slice the leek. Discard the tough stalk ends from the asparagus and cut the stems into 5 cm (2 inch) lengths. Melt 15 g (½ oz) butter in a frying pan and gently fry the leek for about 5 minutes or until it is softened. Add the asparagus, cover with a lid and cook on the lowest heat for 6–7 minutes or until just tender.

❷ Tip the mixture into a food processor and blend to a smooth purée. Blend in the cream and transfer the purée to a small saucepan.

❸ Halve the bacon rashers lengthways and then widthways to make short strips and cook them in a clean frying pan until crisp and golden. Drain and keep warm.

❹ Heat the asparagus purée through gently while you cook the scallops. Add the scallops to the very hot frying pan, sprinkle with a little seasoning and cook for 2–3 minutes on each side.

❺ Spoon the purée on to serving plates and arrange the scallops with the bacon on top. Melt the remaining butter in the pan and drizzle over the scallops. Serve sprinkled with chervil or parsley.

Red mullet tartlets with sauce vièrge

The combination of red mullet, tomatoes and colourful, herby sauce is really stunning in these little pastries.

Preparation time 25 minutes
Cooking time 30 minutes
Serves 6

8 red mullet fillets
2 tablespoons extra virgin olive oil
400 g (13 oz) puff pastry (see page 48), thawed if frozen
1 egg yolk, to glaze
350 g (11½ oz) cherry tomatoes, halved
salt and pepper
1 quantity Sauce Vièrge (see page 162), to serve

❶ Season the red mullet fillets. Heat the oil in a large frying pan and fry the fillets briefly on both sides. Slice the fish into chunky pieces.

❷ Make the sauce vièrge, following the instructions on page 162.

❸ Roll out the pastry on a lightly floured surface and cut out 6 rounds, each 12 cm (5 inches) across, using a cutter or small bowl as a guide. Place them on a lightly greased baking sheet and use the tip of a sharp knife to make a shallow cut 1 cm (½ inch) from the edge of each round. Brush the rims with egg yolk. Bake in a preheated oven, 220°C (425°F), Gas Mark 7, for 15 minutes or until well risen and golden. Scoop out the risen centres of the pastries.

❹ Pile the tomatoes and fish into the tartlets and return to the oven for a further 10 minutes. Meanwhile, gently heat the sauce. Transfer the tartlets to serving plates and spoon some sauce over each.

Crispy duck tarts

These individual tarts have a distinctly oriental flavour partly because of the hoisin sauce, which is a common ingredient in many Southeast Asian dishes.

Preparation time 45 minutes, plus chilling

Cooking time 55 minutes

Serves 6

375 g (12 oz) puff pastry (see page 48), thawed if frozen

beaten egg or milk, to glaze

2 duck legs

6 tablespoons crème fraîche

8 tablespoons hoisin sauce

6 spring onions, thinly sliced

½ cucumber, cut into matchsticks

15 g (½ oz) coriander leaves

1 Roll out the pastry on a lightly floured surface and cut it into 6 squares, each 10 x 10 cm (4 x 4 inches). Make 2 L-shaped cuts in the pastry 2.5 cm (1 inch) in from the edge, leaving the 2 opposite corners uncut. Brush the edges of each pastry square with water.

2 Lift up a cut corner and draw it across the pastry to the opposite cut side. Repeat with the other cut side to form a case. Brush the edges of the pastry with egg or milk, prick the base with a fork, put on a lightly oiled baking sheet and chill.

3 Meanwhile, prick the duck legs with a fork and place them on a rack over a baking tin to catch the fat. Roast in a preheated oven, 200°C (400°F), Gas Mark 6, for 30 minutes. Leave to cool, then shred the meat and skin from the duck legs. Leave the oven on.

4 Put the meat in a bowl with the crème fraîche and hoisin sauce, mix well and divide among the bases of the prepared tarts. Bake for 25 minutes until the pastry has risen and is golden on top.

5 Mix together the spring onion, cucumber and coriander and arrange the mixture on top of the tarts just before serving. The tarts may be eaten hot or cold.

Spicy crab tartlets

These dainty tartlets are filled with a wonderful combination of Asian flavours. They are surprisingly easy to make and make excellent party canapés.

Preparation time 10–12 minutes, plus chilling
Cooking time 10–12 minutes
Makes 12 tartlets

375 g (12 oz) shortcrust pastry (see page 46), thawed if frozen

125 g (4 oz) fresh white crab meat

1 ripe tomato, peeled, deseeded and finely chopped

1 small garlic clove, crushed

2 tablespoons chopped coriander leaves, plus extra for garnishing

¼–½ teaspoon ground cayenne

4 tablespoons mayonnaise

dash of lemon juice

salt and pepper

1 Roll out the pastry thinly on a lightly floured board and use a 6 cm (2½ inch) cutter to stamp out 12 circles. Line the sections of a bun tin with the pastry, prick the base of each one with a fork and chill for 15 minutes. Bake in a preheated oven, 200°C (400°F), Gas Mark 6, for 10–12 minutes until lightly golden. Leave to cool.

2 Carefully fork through the crab meat to remove any small pieces of cartilage that may remain.

3 Add the tomato, garlic, coriander, cayenne and mayonnaise to the crab. Add a little lemon juice and season to taste with salt and pepper.

4 Fill the tartlet cases with the crab mixture, garnish with coriander and serve.

Marinated herring and haricot beans

This is a good snack or starter to make when you see really fresh, plump herrings. Immersed in a tangy marinade that helps preserve the fish, this keeps in the refrigerator for three days.

Preparation time 10 minutes, plus cooling
Cooking time 3 minutes
Serves 4

4 herrings, filleted
200 ml (7 fl oz) cider vinegar
2 teaspoons sea salt
4 tablespoons caster sugar
1 teaspoon coriander seeds, crushed
1 teaspoon mustard seeds, crushed
pinch of ground allspice
2 bay leaves
2 salad onions or 4 spring onions, shredded
410 g (13½ oz) can haricot beans, rinsed and drained
4 tablespoons chopped parsley
1 tablespoon chopped mint
crusty bread, to serve

1 Cut each herring fillet in half and scatter them in a shallow, non-metallic dish.

2 Put the vinegar, salt, sugar, spices and bay leaves in a saucepan and bring just to the boil, stirring until the sugar has dissolved.

3 Pour the marinade over the fish and set it aside to cool completely.

4 Stir in the salad or spring onions, beans, parsley and mint. Cover and chill for up to 3 days. Serve with crusty bread for mopping up the juices.

Chorizo-stuffed plaice with tomatoes

Chorizo sausage makes a fabulous filling for white fish, giving it instant Mediterranean appeal. Any other small flat fish, such as halibut or lemon sole, can also be used.

Preparation time 20 minutes
Cooking time 25 minutes
Serves 4

100 g (3½ oz) piece chorizo sausage
50 g (2 oz) breadcrumbs
2 tablespoons sun-dried tomato paste
5 tablespoons olive oil
8 skinned fillets of 2 large plaice
8 small ripe tomatoes or 4 large tomatoes, halved
several sprigs of thyme
splash of white wine
salt and pepper

1 Cut the chorizo into pieces and blend in a food processor until it is finely chopped. Add the breadcrumbs, tomato paste and 1 tablespoon oil and blend until combined.

2 Lay the plaice fillets, skinned side up, on the work surface. Spread each with a thin layer of the chorizo mixture.

3 Starting from the thick end, roll up the fillet with the chorizo mixture inside.

4 Put the fish in a large, shallow, ovenproof dish and tuck the tomatoes and thyme around the fish. Drizzle with the remaining oil and the wine and season the fish lightly.

5 Bake in a preheated oven, 200°C (400°F), Gas Mark 6, for 20–25 minutes or until cooked through.

Chicken, mushroom and pasta frittata

This creamy, cheesy dish is rather like a deep, baked omelette, ideal for cutting into wedges and serving with salad.

Preparation time 20 minutes
Cooking time 30 minutes
Serves 4

150 g (5 oz) dried pappardelle or other wide ribbon noodles

2 skinless chicken breasts, about 300 g (10 oz) in total, thinly sliced

25 g (1 oz) butter

1 tablespoon olive oil

200 g (7 oz) chestnut mushrooms, sliced

6 eggs

150 ml (¼ pint) double cream

75 g (3 oz) Parmesan cheese, grated

3 tablespoons chopped tarragon

2 tablespoons chopped parsley

salt and pepper

1. Boil the pasta for 6–8 minutes or until just tender. Drain and return to the pan. Season the chicken lightly. Melt the butter with the oil in a heavy-based frying pan and gently fry the chicken for 5 minutes or until cooked through. Remove with a slotted spoon and add the mushrooms to the pan. Fry for 5 minutes or until the moisture has evaporated.

2. Beat together the eggs, cream and half the Parmesan in a large bowl.

3. Toss the pasta with the chicken, mushrooms and herbs and pile into a frying pan with an ovenproof handle.

4. Pour over the egg mixture and heat gently for a couple of minutes until it starts to set. Sprinkle with the remaining Parmesan and transfer to a preheated oven, 180°C (350°F), Gas Mark 4, for 15–20 minutes or until lightly set.

5. Remove the frittata from the oven and allow it to cool slightly before serving.

Smoked salmon ravioli with dill cream sauce

Japanese wasabi paste is a hot, fragrant horseradish, but you can use ordinary horseradish, or half and half, if you prefer.

Preparation time 50 minutes, plus standing

Cooking time 15 minutes

Serves 6

175 g (6 oz) smoked salmon

1½ teaspoons wasabi paste

75 g (3 oz) ricotta cheese

1 quantity pasta dough (see page 24)

150 ml (¼ pint) fish stock

150 ml (¼ pint) white wine

150 ml (¼ pint) double cream

4 tablespoons chopped dill

salt and pepper

1 Finely chop the salmon and place it in a bowl with the wasabi paste and ricotta. Beat well until evenly mixed.

2 Use the pasta dough and smoked salmon mixture to make the ravioli, following the method on page 26.

3 Once the ravioli has been shaped and left to dry for 30 minutes, bring a large saucepan of salted water to the boil and cook it in 2–3 batches for 4–5 minutes (once the water has returned to the boil), until they are just tender.

4 Meanwhile, stir the cream and dill into the reduced stock and heat until bubbling around the edges. Season to taste with salt and pepper. Drain the ravioli and serve in warm shallow dishes with the sauce.

Chicken liver and herb pâté

Chicken livers are brilliant for pâté – they are quick to cook and blend to a smooth, creamy consistency. Packed under a buttery seal, the pâté will keep for several days in the refrigerator.

Preparation time 10 minutes, plus chilling
Cooking time 10 minutes
Serves 5–6

500 g (1 lb) chicken livers
125 g (4 oz) butter, softened
1 onion, chopped
2 tablespoons sherry or Marsala
3 pickled onions, drained and finely chopped
1 tablespoon capers, rinsed, drained and finely chopped
2 teaspoons chopped dill
salt and pepper

❶ Wash the chicken livers, drain well and pat them dry on kitchen paper.

❷ Melt 50 g (2 oz) butter in a large, heavy-based frying pan until it is bubbling. Add the onion and fry gently until softened. Add the chicken livers and fry for about 10 minutes, stirring until just cooked through.

❸ Stir the sherry or Marsala into the mixture in the pan.

❹ Tip the liver mixture into a food processor or blender and blend until smooth and creamy, scraping the mixture down from the sides of the bowl if necessary. Stir in the chopped pickled onions, capers and dill and season to taste.

❺ Pack the pâté into individual serving dishes or into a large pâté dish and press it down in an even layer. Melt the remaining butter and pour it over the surface of the pâté. Cover and chill for at least 2 hours before serving with crisp, toast slices.

Pork, prosciutto and pepper terrine

A colourful mixture of meat, peppers and herbs packed in a delicious jellied stock is great for a starter or picnic dish. Serve with herb salad and warm bread.

Preparation time 30 minutes, plus chilling
Cooking time 1½ hours
Serves 6–8

1 tablespoon vegetable oil
1 kg (2 lb) piece shoulder of pork, skinned
1 glass of white wine
3 red peppers, deseeded and quartered
75 g (3 oz) smoked back bacon, roughly chopped
25 g (1 oz) flat leaf parsley
15 g (½ oz) coriander
75 g (3 oz) pine nuts, toasted
2 teaspoons Tabasco sauce
300 ml (½ pint) jellied Veal Stock (see page 18)
salt and pepper

1 Heat the oil in a roasting tin and sear the pork on all sides. Pour over the wine and cover the tin with foil. Bake in a preheated oven, 180°C (350°F), Gas Mark 4, for 1 hour. Add the peppers and bacon to the tin and return to the oven, uncovered, for a further 30 minutes until the meat is cooked through. Drain the meat and peppers, reserving the pan juices. Leave to cool.

2 Cut the meat into pieces, discarding any excess fat. Use a food processor to chop the meat finely. Do this in 2–3 batches. Tip into a bowl. Chop the peppers and bacon into small pieces and finely chop the parsley and coriander.

3 Add the chopped peppers, bacon and herbs to the pork with the pine nuts, Tabasco sauce and seasoning and mix well. Pack into a 1 kg (2 lb) pâté dish.

4 Skim the fat off the meat roasting juices and tip the juices into a small pan with the veal stock. Reheat gently until liquid. Leave until cold but not jellied then pour the stock over the pork. Cover and chill for several hours or overnight.

PASTA, RICE AND NOODLES

Linguine with shredded ham and eggs

Like so many pasta dishes, this recipe is put together in minutes and is conveniently adaptable. Use other cooked meats or throw in small amounts of other additions, such as capers or herbs.

Preparation time 5 minutes

Cooking time 10 minutes

Serves 2

3 tablespoons chopped flat leaf parsley

1 tablespoon grainy mustard

2 teaspoons lemon juice

good pinch of caster sugar

3 tablespoons olive oil

100 g (3½ oz) ham

2 spring onions

2 eggs

125 g (4 oz) dried linguine

salt and pepper

1. Bring a saucepan of lightly salted water to the boil to cook the pasta. Meanwhile, mix together the parsley, mustard, lemon juice, sugar, oil and a little salt and pepper.

2. Roll up the ham and slice it as thinly as possible.

3. Trim the spring onions, cut them lengthways into thin shreds, then cut across into 5 cm (2 inch) lengths.

4. Put the eggs in a small saucepan and just cover with cold water. Bring to the boil and cook for 4 minutes (once the water boils the eggs will start moving around).

5. Put the pasta in the salted water, return to the boil and boil for 6–8 minutes or until just tender. Add the spring onions and cook for a further 30 seconds.

6. Drain the pasta and return to the pan. Stir in the ham and the mustard dressing and pile on to warm serving plates. Shell and halve the eggs and serve on top.

Spaghetti carbonara

The heat from the steaming hot spaghetti lightly cooks the creamy egg sauce. This is a quickly assembled dish, so have everything ready before you begin.

Preparation time 10 minutes
Cooking time 5 minutes
Serves 4

4 egg yolks
2 eggs
150 ml (¼ pint) single cream
50 g (2 oz) Parmesan cheese, grated
2 tablespoons olive oil
100 g (3½ oz) pancetta or streaky bacon, finely sliced
2 garlic cloves, crushed
400 g (13 oz) fresh or dried spaghetti
salt and pepper

❶ Beat together the egg yolks, whole eggs, cream, Parmesan and plenty of pepper.

❷ Heat the oil in a large frying pan and fry the pancetta or bacon for 3–4 minutes or until golden and turning crisp. Add the garlic and cook for 1 minute further.

❸ Meanwhile, bring a large saucepan of lightly salted water to the boil, add the spaghetti and cook for 2 minutes or until tender.

❹ Drain the spaghetti and immediately tip it into the frying pan. Turn off the heat and stir in the egg mixture until the eggs are lightly cooked. Serve immediately. (If the heat of the pasta doesn't quite cook the egg sauce, turn on the heat and cook briefly, stirring.)

Goats' cheese and pepper lasagne

Meat-free lasagnes can be just as flavour packed as meaty ones. The creamy goats' cheese sauce is lovely against the tangy flavours of the peppers.

Preparation time 30 minutes, plus soaking and cooling
Cooking time 1 hour
Serves 4–5

50 g (2 oz) dried porcini mushrooms
225 g (7½ oz) spinach
4 tablespoons olive oil
1 large onion, sliced
2 red peppers, deseeded and roughly chopped
3 garlic cloves, sliced
2 x 400 g (13 oz) cans chopped tomatoes
4 tablespoons sun-dried tomato pesto
2 tablespoons chopped oregano
300 g (10 oz) soft goats' cheese
1 quantity Béchamel Sauce (see page 20)
200 g (7 oz) dried lasagne sheets
50 g (2 oz) breadcrumbs
salt and pepper

❶ Soak the mushrooms in 200 ml (7 fl oz) boiling water. Wilt the spinach. Heat 2 tablespoons oil in a saucepan and fry the onion and red peppers for 5 minutes. Add the garlic, tomatoes, pesto, oregano, spinach, mushrooms and their soaking liquid and salt and pepper. Bring to the boil and simmer gently for 10 minutes.

❷ Beat the goats' cheese into the béchamel sauce. Spoon one-quarter of the vegetable sauce into a shallow, 1.5 litre (2½ pint) ovenproof dish. Spread with one-quarter of the béchamel sauce.

❸ Arrange one-third of the pasta sheets over the sauce, trimming or breaking them to fit.

❹ Repeat the layering, finishing with béchamel sauce. Toss the breadcrumbs with the remaining oil and scatter over the sauce. Bake in a preheated oven, 190°C (375°F), Gas Mark 5, for 45 minutes or until crisp and golden.

Silhouette pasta with lemon sole

This recipe sandwiches fragrant herb leaves between wafer-thin sheets of homemade pasta, creating a stunning silhouette effect.

Preparation time 45 minutes, plus drying

Cooking time 10 minutes

Serves 4

1 quantity pasta dough
(see page 24)

about 15 g (½ oz) small leaf herbs, such as basil, tarragon, chervil or flat leaf parsley

100 g (3½ oz) butter

2 large lemon sole, filleted, skinned and cut into chunks

2 tablespoons salted capers

1 tablespoon lemon juice

salt and pepper

1 Line 2 trays with flour-dusted tea towels or kitchen paper. Thinly roll out the pasta dough, using a machine or by hand (see page 25). Very lightly brush one sheet of dough with water and arrange the leaves over the dough.

2 Lay another sheet of rolled dough over the pasta and press down gently. Repeat with the remaining pasta sheets.

3 Reroll the dough, again using the machine or by hand, until it is fine enough to see the herbs clearly through the pasta.

4 Cut the sheet of pasta into 2.5 cm (1 inch) wide strips. Transfer the strips to the trays and leave to dry for 30 minutes.

5 Bring a large pan of lightly salted water to the boil. Melt half the butter in a frying pan. Season the fish with salt and pepper and fry gently for 3–4 minutes. Add the capers.

6 Put the pasta in the boiling water, return to the boil and cook for 2 minutes until tender. Drain, return to the pan and gently toss with the fish and capers. Pile on to warm serving plates. Melt the remaining butter in the frying pan and stir in the lemon juice. Season and drizzle over the pasta.

Seared tuna with angel hair pasta

Of all the long pastas, vermicelli has the finest strands and is sometimes referred to as *capelli d'angelo* (angel hair).

Preparation time 10 minutes, plus marinating
Cooking time 10 minutes
Serves 4

100 ml (3½ fl oz) olive oil
2 garlic cloves, crushed
finely grated rind and juice of 1 lime
500 g (1 lb) tuna, in one piece
1 bunch of spring onions, sliced
4 tablespoons chopped dill or fennel
2 tablespoons coarse grain mustard
2 teaspoons caster sugar
4 tablespoons single cream
200 g (7 oz) fine vermicelli
salt and pepper
lime wedges, to serve

1. Mix 1 tablespoon oil with the garlic, lime rind and juice and plenty of pepper. Put the tuna in a non-metallic dish, spoon over the marinade and cover. Chill for 30 minutes.

2. Heat 2 tablespoons oil in a frying pan and fry the spring onions for 1 minute. Remove with a slotted spoon. Add the tuna to the pan and fry gently, turning frequently, until deep golden but still pink in the centre. This will take about 10 minutes. (Test by slicing off the end: it should still be pink in the centre.)

3. Meanwhile, bring a large saucepan of lightly salted water to the boil, ready to cook the pasta. Beat the remaining oil with the dill or fennel, mustard, sugar and cream.

4. Tip the pasta into the boiling water and cook for 3 minutes or until tender. Drain and return to the pan. Stir in half the dressing and the spring onions and pile on to warm plates.

5. Thinly slice the tuna and place on top. Spoon over the remaining dressing and serve with lime wedges.

Spicy sausage bake

Make this quick and easy supper dish with the most garlicky, spicy sausages you can find. Their flavour will mingle with all the other ingredients as they cook.

Preparation time 15 minutes

Cooking time 45 minutes

Serves 4

450 g (14½ oz) Italian sausages

2 tablespoons olive oil

1 large red onion, sliced

2 x 400 g (13 oz) cans chopped tomatoes

2 tablespoons chopped oregano

400 g (13 oz) can red kidney beans, drained and rinsed

200 g (7 oz) dried fusilli

175 g (6 oz) fontina cheese, grated

salt and pepper

1. Slice each sausage into quarters. Heat the oil in a large, heavy-based frying pan and gently fry the sausages and onion for about 10 minutes until golden, gently shaking the pan frequently.

2. Add the tomatoes, oregano and red kidney beans. Reduce the heat to its lowest setting and cook gently for 10 minutes.

3. Meanwhile, cook the pasta in plenty of boiling, salted water for about 10 minutes or until just tender. Drain and tip into the frying pan.

4. Add half the fontina and toss the ingredients together until mixed.

5. Tip into a 1.5 litre (2½ pint) shallow ovenproof dish and scatter with the remaining fontina. Bake in a preheated oven, 200°C (400°F), Gas Mark 6, for 20–25 minutes or until the cheese is melting and golden.

Mushroom tagliatelle with gremolata

Gremolata is a mixture of herbs, lemon rind and garlic. It's used to bring a burst of lively, aromatic flavour to this dish.

Preparation time 30 minutes, plus drying
Cooking time 10 minutes
Serves 4

1 quantity mushroom-flavoured pasta dough (see page 25)
15 g (½ oz) dried porcini mushrooms
50 g (2 oz) butter
4 tablespoons olive oil
1 small onion, finely chopped
200 g (7 oz) chestnut or button mushrooms, thinly sliced
4 tablespoons chopped herbs, such as parsley, tarragon, fennel or basil
finely grated rind of 1 lemon
2 garlic cloves, finely chopped
salt and pepper
Parmesan cheese, grated, to serve (optional)

1 Use the pasta dough to make tagliatelle (see page 26). Leave to dry. Put the porcini mushrooms in a bowl, cover with boiling water and leave to stand for 15 minutes. Melt the butter with 1 tablespoon oil in a frying pan and fry the onion for 3 minutes or until softened. Drain the soaked mushrooms and thinly slice them.

2 Add the porcini mushrooms to the pan with the chestnut or button mushrooms and a quarter of the herbs. Fry gently for 5 minutes. Mix the remaining herbs with the lemon rind, garlic and plenty of black pepper.

3 Bring a large saucepan of salted water to the boil. Add the pasta, return to the boil and cook for about 2 minutes until tender.

4 Drain the pasta and return to the saucepan. Add the mixture from the frying pan and toss the ingredients with the remaining oil. Transfer to warm serving plates and serve with the gremolata.

Tagliatelle with spicy pea fritters

These little split pea fritters are quite hot and spicy, so halve the spices for a milder flavour. They can be made in advance and kept in the refrigerator.

Preparation time 30 minutes, plus soaking
Cooking time 40 minutes
Serves 4

300 g (10 oz) split yellow peas
1 onion, roughly chopped
25 g (1 oz) breadcrumbs
2 garlic cloves, chopped
1 tablespoon crushed cumin seeds
¾ teaspoon dried chilli flakes
several sprigs of mint
1 egg
8 tablespoons lemon-infused olive oil
25 g (1 oz) butter
200 g (7 oz) dried tagliatelle
200 g (7 oz) roasted red peppers, thinly sliced
4 tablespoons chopped coriander
salt and pepper

1 Put the peas in a large bowl, cover them with cold water and leave to soak overnight. Drain and put them in a saucepan. Cover with cold water, bring to the boil and cook for about 25 minutes or until tender. Drain. Tip the peas into a food processor with the onion, breadcrumbs, garlic, cumin seeds, chilli, mint, egg and salt and pepper and blend to a smooth paste.

2 Shape the pea mixture firmly into small balls, about 2.5 cm (1 inch) in diameter.

3 Bring a large saucepan of lightly salted water to the boil, ready to cook the pasta. Heat half the oil with the butter in a large frying pan. Add the pea fritters and fry gently, stirring, for 5 minutes or until golden.

4 Add the pasta to the water, return to the boil and cook for about 10 minutes or until just tender. Drain and return to the saucepan. Stir in the peppers, coriander, pea fritters and remaining oil and mix together gently to serve.

Gnocchi with broad beans and Parmesan

This is a potato-based gnocchi, which is shaped traditionally into grooved nuggets and dressed up with beans and crispy bacon.

Preparation time 10 minutes

Cooking time 15 minutes

Serves 4–6

1 quantity Gnocchi (see page 27)

50 g (2 oz) butter, plus extra for greasing

200 g (7 oz) baby broad beans

2 tablespoons olive oil

75 g (3 oz) smoked bacon or pancetta, finely chopped

40 g (1½ oz) Parmesan cheese, grated

salt and pepper

❶ Make, shape and cook the gnocchi. Once drained, tip them into a shallow, lightly buttered ovenproof dish or 4–6 individual dishes.

❷ Blanch the beans in boiling water for 2 minutes. Drain thoroughly and scatter over and around the gnocchi.

❸ Melt the butter with the oil in a frying pan and fry the bacon or pancetta until crisp and golden. Spoon over the gnocchi and drizzle over the juices in the pan.

❹ Sprinkle with the Parmesan and bake in a preheated oven, 200°C (400°F), Gas Mark 6, for 10–15 minutes to heat through.

Aubergine cannelloni

Although it is a little fiddly to prepare, this dish is well worth the effort, making a delicious combination of creamy ricotta filling and sweet, grilled aubergines.

Preparation time 45 minutes

Cooking time 1 hour

Serves 4

1 quantity Roasted Tomato Sauce (see page 23)

4 sheets fresh or dried lasagne, each about 18 x 15 cm (7 x 6 inches)

2 medium aubergines, thinly sliced

4 tablespoons olive oil

1 teaspoon finely chopped thyme

250 g (8 oz) ricotta cheese

25 g (1 oz) basil leaves, torn into pieces

2 garlic cloves, crushed

100 g (3½ oz) fontina or Gruyère cheese, grated

salt and pepper

1 Make the roasted tomato sauce. Bring a saucepan of salted water to the boil. Add the lasagne sheets, return to the boil and cook, allowing 2 minutes for fresh and 8–10 minutes for dried. Drain the sheets and immerse them in cold water. Place the aubergines in a single layer on a foil-lined grill rack. (You may need to do this in 2 batches.) Mix the olive oil, thyme and seasoning and brush over the aubergines. Grill until lightly browned, turning once.

2 Mix the ricotta, with the basil, garlic and seasoning. Beat together.

3 Thoroughly drain the pasta sheets and lay them on the work surface. Cut each in half. Spread the ricotta mixture over the sheets, right to the edges. Arrange the aubergine slices on top. Roll up each piece.

4 Spread two-thirds of the tomato sauce in a shallow ovenproof dish and arrange the cannelloni on top. Spoon over the remaining tomato sauce and sprinkle with the cheese. Bake in a preheated oven, 190°C (375°F), Gas Mark 5, for 20 minutes or until golden.

Pumpkin ravioli

The filling for this dish is delicious but very soft and creamy, so it is not a good 'make-ahead' dish because the pumpkin will gradually dampen the pasta.

Preparation time 40 minutes, plus drying
Cooking time 50 minutes
Serves 4

450 g (14½ oz) pumpkin or squash, cut into small chunks, skin and seeds discarded

3 tablespoons olive oil

½ small onion, finely chopped

1 garlic clove, crushed

25 g (1 oz) amaretti biscuits, crushed

50 g (2 oz) cream cheese

plenty of freshly grated nutmeg

1 quantity pasta dough (see page 24)

flour, for dusting

75 g (3 oz) butter

1 teaspoon finely chopped rosemary

2 tablespoons chopped parsley

finely grated rind of 1 lemon and 1 tablespoon juice

salt and pepper

❶ Put the pumpkin or squash into a roasting tin and drizzle with half the oil. Roast in a preheated oven, 200°C (400°F), Gas Mark 6, for 30–40 minutes until tender.

❷ Heat the remaining oil in a frying pan and fry the onion until softened. Add the garlic and fry for a further 1 minute. Mash the cooled pumpkin in a bowl until pulpy. Beat in the onion, garlic, crushed biscuits, cream cheese and nutmeg. (Alternatively, whizz the lot together in a food processor.) Check the seasoning.

❸ Line 2 trays with flour-dusted tea towels or kitchen paper. Roll out the pasta (see page 25). Use the dough and pumpkin mixture to make ravioli, following the method on page 26. Leave on the floured trays to dry for 30 minutes before cooking.

❹ Melt the butter in a saucepan and stir in the herbs, lemon rind and juice and pepper. Bring a large pan of salted water to the boil. Cook in batches, for 3–5 minutes. Drain well and pile on warm serving plates.

Buckwheat fusilli with tofu, pumpkin and sugar snap peas

Buckwheat pasta provides texture, flavour and colour contrast. For a change substitute thinly sliced chicken breasts for the tofu.

Preparation time 15 minutes
Cooking time 15 minutes
Serves 2

250 g (8 oz) tofu
2 tablespoons vegetable oil
3 garlic cloves, crushed
1 hot red chilli, deseeded and chopped
1 bunch of spring onions, sliced into 1.5 cm (¾ inch) lengths
100 g (3½ oz) sugar snap peas, each sliced into 3
300 g (10 oz) pumpkin, deseeded, skinned and cut into
5 mm–5 cm (¼–2 inch) sticks
150 g (5 oz) buckwheat fusilli

Dressing
½ teaspoon cornflour
4 tablespoons mirin
1 tablespoon caster sugar
1 tablespoon (1 sachet) miso soup paste
2 tablespoons toasted sesame oil
2 tablespoons light soy sauce

❶ Make the dressing by blending the cornflour with 1 tablespoon water in a small bowl. Add the mirin, sugar, miso paste, sesame oil and soy sauce. Bring a large saucepan of lightly salted water to the boil, ready to cook the fusilli. Drain the tofu and pat dry on kitchen paper. Cut it into small chunks.

❷ Heat the oil in a frying pan or wok. Add the garlic and chilli and fry for 15 seconds. Add the tofu, spring onions, peas and pumpkin and stir-fry for 8–10 minutes or until the vegetables have softened but retain a little texture.

❸ Meanwhile, cook the pasta in the water for about 10 minutes or until tender. Drain through a colander and tip into the pan with the vegetables and tofu.

❹ Stir the dressing, add to the pan and cook for 1 minute, tossing the ingredients together until heated through.

Arancini

These little risotto fritters are flavoured with basil and mozzarella and fried so they are crisp on the outside and meltingly soft inside. Serve as a snack with grilled pork or lamb.

Preparation time 30 minutes, plus cooling
Cooking time 45 minutes
Serves 4

50 g (2 oz) butter
1 onion, finely chopped
2 garlic cloves, crushed
250 g (8 oz) risotto rice
small glass white wine
600 ml (1 pint) hot Chicken or Vegetable Stock (see pages 18–19)
½ teaspoon saffron strands
50 g (2 oz) Parmesan cheese, grated
25 g (1 oz) basil leaves, torn into small pieces
150 g (5 oz) mozzarella cheese, cut into 1 cm (½ inch) dice
75 g (3 oz) breadcrumbs
vegetable oil, for deep frying

1 Melt the butter in a large, heavy-based saucepan. Fry the onion gently for 5 minutes until softened. Add the garlic and rice and cook, stirring, for 1 minute.

2 Add the wine and let the mixture bubble until the wine evaporates, then add the stock and saffron and bring to the boil. Reduce the heat and simmer gently, uncovered, until the stock has been absorbed and the rice is tender. (Add a little boiling water to the pan if the stock evaporates before the rice is tender.) Turn the risotto into a bowl, stir in the Parmesan and basil and leave until completely cold.

3 Form a dessertspoonful of the mixture into a cake in your hands and press a cube of mozzarella into the centre. Roll into a ball so the cheese is enclosed by the risotto mixture. Repeat with the remaining mixture, then roll each fritter lightly in the breadcrumbs.

4 Heat oil to a depth of 5 cm (2 inch) in a deep-fat fryer or large saucepan until a few breadcrumbs sizzle on the surface. Fry the arancini, in batches, for 4–5 minutes or until they are crisp and golden. Drain on kitchen paper and keep warm while you cook the rest.

Kipper kedgeree

Although it is usually made with smoked haddock, kedgeree adapts well to almost any smoked fish, so look out for the best deal when you are shopping.

Preparation time 15 minutes

Cooking time 15 minutes

Serves 4

250 g (8 oz) basmati rice

4 eggs

625 g (1¼ lb) kippers

2 teaspoons fennel seeds

8 cardamom pods

25 g (1 oz) butter

1 onion, finely chopped

1 teaspoon ground turmeric

1 cinnamon stick

4 tablespoons chopped parsley

salt and pepper

lemon or lime wedges, to serve

❶ Cook the rice in plenty of boiling water for about 10 minutes or until tender. Put the eggs in a separate saucepan, cover with freshly boiled water and bring to the boil. Simmer gently for 5 minutes. Drain the rice and eggs. Meanwhile, put the kippers in a frying pan, just cover with hot water and simmer gently for 5 minutes. Drain.

❷ When the fish is cool enough to handle, roughly flake the flesh, discarding the skin and bones. Shell and quarter the boiled eggs.

❸ Use a pestle and mortar to crush the fennel seeds and cardamom pods. Remove the cardamom pods, leaving the seeds.

❹ Melt the butter in a frying pan and gently fry the onion and all the spices for 5 minutes. Stir in the rice, fish, eggs and parsley and season to taste. Serve with lemon or lime wedges.

Monkfish and saffron risotto

Monkfish is an excellent choice for risotto. Firm and meaty in texture, it can be stirred into the creamy rice without breaking up into little flakes.

Preparation time 25 minutes
Cooking time 25 minutes
Serves 3–4

500 g (1 lb) monkfish, boned
50 g (2 oz) butter
1 onion, chopped
2 garlic cloves, crushed
250 g (8 oz) risotto rice
1 glass dry white wine
1 teaspoon saffron strands
2 teaspoons chopped lemon thyme, plus extra to serve
1 litre (1¾ pints) hot Fish Stock (see page 19)
salt and pepper
grated Parmesan cheese, to serve

❶ Cut the monkfish into chunks and season lightly. Melt half the butter in a large, heavy-based saucepan and gently fry the onion until it is softened but not browned. Add the fish and cook, stirring, for 2 minutes. Drain the fish and add the garlic to the pan. Cook for 1 minute.

❷ Sprinkle in the rice and fry gently for 1 minute. Add the wine to the saucepan and let it bubble until almost evaporated.

❸ Add the saffron, thyme and a ladleful of the stock and cook, stirring, until the rice has absorbed the stock. Continue to add the stock, a ladleful at a time, cooking the rice and stirring until the stock is almost absorbed between each addition.

❹ After about 20 minutes check the consistency of the rice. It should be creamy and tender but slightly firm in the centre. (You might not need all the stock.) Check the seasoning and stir in the fish. Heat through and serve immediately, scattered with Parmesan and chopped thyme.

Sushi

This simplified version of rolled sushi is similar in flavour to the authentic version but takes half the time. Use any mixture of fish as long as you can be sure that it's absolutely fresh.

Preparation time 30 minutes, plus cooling
Cooking time 15 minutes
Serves 4–6

225 g (7½ oz) Japanese sushi rice
4 spring onions, very finely shredded
4 tablespoons seasoned rice vinegar
1 tablespoon caster sugar
25 g (1 oz) pickled ginger, shredded
1 tablespoon toasted sesame seeds
100 g (3½ oz) wild salmon
1 large sole fillet
3–4 sheets of nori
10 peeled cooked prawns
light soy sauce, to serve

❶ Put the rice in a heavy-based saucepan with 450 ml (¾ pint) water. Bring slowly to the boil, then reduce the heat and simmer, half-covered with a lid, for 5–8 minutes or until all the water is absorbed. Cover completely and cook very gently for 5 minutes or until the rice is tender and sticky. Turn into a bowl and leave to cool.

❷ Stir the spring onions, rice vinegar, sugar, ginger and sesame seeds into the rice. Slice the salmon and sole into small strips.

❸ Use scissors to cut the nori sheets into 6 cm (2½ inch) squares. Dampen your hands and mould the rice into little ovals. Arrange the rice ovals diagonally over the nori squares.

❹ Bring the pointed ends on opposite sides of the nori over the rice and arrange a piece of fish or a prawn on top. Arrange on a serving platter and serve with a small bowl of soy sauce for dipping.

Shellfish laksa

A laksa is an Asian one-pot dish of seafood and noodles in a spicy coconut broth. This version makes a great supper dish, or you can serve smaller portions as an appetizer.

Preparation time 20 minutes
Cooking time 15 minutes
Serves 4

1 hot red chilli, deseeded and sliced
1 stalk of lemon grass, thinly sliced
1 onion, roughly chopped
50 g (2 oz) fresh root ginger, roughly chopped
50 g (2 oz) unsalted roasted peanuts
4 teaspoons Thai fish sauce
3 tablespoons groundnut oil or mild olive oil
8 shelled scallops (see page 39), halved if large
½ teaspoon ground turmeric
600 ml (1 pint) Fish Stock (see page 19)
400 ml (14 fl oz) can coconut milk
150 g (5 oz) dried egg noodles
200 g (7 oz) raw peeled prawns
150 g (5 oz) white crab meat
150 g (5 oz) bean sprouts
15 g (½ oz) fresh coriander, chopped

❶ Put the chilli, lemon grass, onion, ginger, peanuts and fish sauce in a food processor and blend to make a thick paste.

❷ Heat the oil in a large, heavy-based saucepan and gently fry the scallops until they are seared on all sides. Drain with a slotted spoon.

❸ Add the paste to the pan and fry gently, stirring, for 5 minutes. Add the turmeric, stock and coconut milk and bring slowly to a simmer.

❹ Cook the noodles in a separate saucepan until they are tender, following the instructions on the packet.

❺ Meanwhile, stir the prawns and scallops into the broth and cook gently for 3 minutes or until the prawns have turned pink. Stir in the crab meat, bean sprouts and coriander and cook for 1 minute. Drain the noodles, pile them into warm bowls, top with the laksa and serve.

Red rice pilaf with fruit and nuts

Red rice is a fabulous colour and adds a nutty, slightly chewy texture to a pilaf. It is well worth trying if you're unfamiliar with it.

Preparation time 25 minutes
Cooking time about 50 minutes
Serves 4

50 g (2 oz) wild rice
10 cardamom pods
2 teaspoons cumin seeds
2 teaspoons fennel seeds
4 tablespoons olive oil
25 g (1 oz) flaked almonds
2 red onions, thinly sliced
1 teaspoon caster sugar
½ teaspoon ground turmeric
2 garlic cloves, thinly sliced
250 g (8 oz) red rice
600 ml (1 pint) Vegetable Stock (see page 19)
25 g (1 oz) fresh root ginger, grated
6 tablespoons chopped parsley
75 g (3 oz) dried apricots, thinly sliced
250 g (8 oz) ricotta cheese
salt and pepper

① Bring a saucepan of lightly salted water to the boil. Add the wild rice and cook gently for 25–30 minutes or until tender. Crush the cardamom pods using a pestle and mortar to release the seeds. Discard the shells, add the cumin and fennel seeds and lightly crush.

② Heat half the oil in a frying pan and fry the almonds until browned. Drain. Add the remaining oil, onions and sugar and fry for 5 minutes until golden. Drain half and fry the remainder until crisp. Drain on kitchen paper.

③ Return the onions to the pan with the crushed spices, turmeric and garlic and fry for 1 minute. Add the red rice and stock and bring to the boil. Cover with a lid or foil and cook gently for 25–30 minutes or until tender.

④ Stir in the wild rice, ginger, parsley and apricots and season. Dot with teaspoonfuls of ricotta and fold in gently. Serve scattered with the onions and nuts.

Vongole sauce

Small clams, served in a rich tomato sauce and tossed with pasta, make up the classic southern Italian dish, spaghetti vongole. Use linguine or fresh or dried spaghetti.

Preparation time 20 minutes

Cooking time 20 minutes

Serves 4

1 kg (2 lb) small fresh clams

150 ml (¼ pint) dry white wine

4 tablespoons olive oil

1 small onion, finely chopped

3 garlic cloves, crushed

2 x 400 g (13 oz) cans chopped tomatoes

1 teaspoon caster sugar

2 bay leaves

small handful of flat leaf parsley, chopped

finely grated rind and juice of ½ lemon

salt and pepper

1 Scrub the clams, discarding any damaged ones or open ones that do not close when tapped with a knife. Bring the wine to the boil in a large, heavy-based saucepan. Tip in the clams, cover with a tightly fitting lid and cook for 3–4 minutes, shaking the pan frequently until the shells have opened.

2 Remove the clams, reserving the liquor, and shell about half of them, discarding any that remain closed.

3 Heat the oil in the cleaned pan. Add the onion and cook gently for 5 minutes. Add the garlic and cook for a further 1 minute. Add the tomatoes, sugar, bay leaves and the reserved clam liquor and bring to the boil. Reduce the heat and simmer gently for about 10 minutes until the sauce is thickened and pulpy.

4 Stir in the clams, parsley and lemon rind and juice. Heat through for 1 minute. Check the seasoning and serve.

Puttanesca sauce

This intense Italian tomato sauce has plenty of extra flavours, such as black olives, anchovies and chillies. Thick and richly flavoured, it's great tossed with almost any pasta.

Preparation time 15 minutes
Cooking time 15 minutes
Serves 4

4 tablespoons olive oil
1 onion, finely chopped
3 garlic cloves, crushed
1 small red chilli, deseeded and finely chopped
6 anchovy fillets, chopped
2 x 400 g (13 oz) cans chopped tomatoes
½ teaspoon caster sugar
75 g (3 oz) black olives, pitted and finely chopped
small handful of basil leaves
2 tablespoons capers, rinsed and drained
salt
freshly grated Parmesan cheese, to serve (optional)

❶ Heat the oil in a heavy-based saucepan. Add the onion and fry gently for 3–4 minutes or until softened. Add the garlic and chilli and cook for a further minute.

❷ Add the anchovy fillets, tomatoes, sugar and black olives and bring to the boil.

❸ Reduce the heat and simmer gently for 10 minutes or until the sauce has thickened.

❹ Add the basil leaves, capers and a little salt and stir through for 1 minute. Serve hot with spaghetti or linguine, sprinkled with Parmesan cheese, if liked.

Lamb, leek and peppercorn sauce

Use good-quality lamb for this rich, creamy sauce so it's not too watery when you fry it off. Serve with a plain or a spinach-flavoured pasta.

Preparation time 10 minutes
Cooking time 20 minutes
Serves 4

2 leeks
25 g (1 oz) butter
400 g (13 oz) lean minced lamb
2 garlic cloves, crushed
2 teaspoons plain flour
150 ml (¼ pint) Lamb Stock (see page 18) or Vegetable Stock (see page 19)
2 tablespoons green peppercorns in brine, rinsed and drained
100 ml (3½ fl oz) crème fraîche
plenty of freshly grated nutmeg
salt

❶ Trim, rinse and chop the leeks finely.

❷ Melt the butter in a large, shallow pan and gently fry the lamb until it is lightly browned, stirring frequently and breaking up the meat with a wooden spoon. Add the leeks and garlic and fry gently for a further 5 minutes.

❸ Stir in the flour, then the stock and peppercorns and bring the mixture to a gentle simmer. Cover with a lid and cook gently for 10 minutes until the lamb is tender.

❹ Stir in the crème fraîche, plenty of nutmeg and a little salt to taste. Heat through gently before serving.

Bolognese sauce

Bolognese, or ragu, is usually served with tagliatelle rather than spaghetti. It should be thick and pulpy, rather than thin and gravy-like, so it clings to the pasta it's served with.

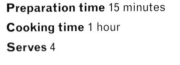

Preparation time 15 minutes
Cooking time 1 hour
Serves 4

15 g (½ oz) butter
3 tablespoons olive oil
1 large onion, finely chopped
1 celery stick, finely chopped
3 garlic cloves, crushed
500 g (1 lb) lean minced beef
150 ml (¼ pint) red wine
2 x 400 g (13 oz) cans chopped tomatoes
2 tablespoons sun-dried tomato paste
3 tablespoons chopped oregano
3 bay leaves
salt and pepper
grated Parmesan cheese, to serve (optional)

❶ Melt the butter with the oil in a large, heavy-based saucepan and gently fry the onion for 5 minutes. Add the celery and fry gently for a further 2 minutes.

❷ Stir in the garlic, then add the minced beef. Fry gently, breaking up the meat, until lightly browned.

❸ Add the wine and let the mixture bubble until the wine reduces slightly.

❹ Stir in the chopped tomatoes, tomato paste, oregano and bay leaves and bring to the boil.

❺ Reduce the heat and cook very gently, uncovered, for about 45 minutes or until the sauce is very thick and pulpy. Check the seasoning and serve with grated Parmesan, if liked.

Pesto

Freshly made pesto has numerous uses, most commonly as a pasta sauce, but it can also be stirred in to flavour soups, stews and risottos.

Preparation time 5 minutes
Serves 4

50 g (2 oz) fresh basil, including stalks
50 g (2 oz) pine nuts
65 g (2½ oz) freshly grated Parmesan cheese
2 garlic cloves, chopped
125 ml (4 fl oz) olive oil
salt and pepper

1 Tear the basil into pieces.

2 Put the basil into a food processor with the pine nuts, Parmesan and garlic.

3 Blend lightly until the nuts and cheese are broken into small pieces, scraping the mixture down from the sides of the bowl if necessary.

4 Add the olive oil and a little salt and blend to a thick paste. Stir into freshly cooked pasta or turn into a bowl and refrigerate. It can be kept, covered, for up to 5 days.

5 Make red pesto by draining and finely chopping 125 g (4 oz) sun-dried tomatoes in oil and adding them to the food processor instead of the basil.

Thai green sauce

With their unique depth of flavour but fresh taste, it's easy to see why Thai-style curries are so popular. The blended paste can be used in traditional recipes or simply stirred through noodles.

Preparation time 10 minutes

Cooking time 25 minutes

Serves 4

2 lemon grass stalks, trimmed and sliced

50 g (2 oz) piece fresh root ginger, peeled and roughly chopped

4 garlic cloves, roughly chopped

1 onion, roughly chopped

2 hot green chillies, deseeded and chopped

large bunch of coriander, about 25 g (1 oz)

½ teaspoon ground turmeric

1 teaspoon ground cumin

2 tablespoons water

1 tablespoon caster sugar

1 tablespoon Thai fish sauce

1 tablespoon lime juice

400 ml (14 fl oz) can coconut milk

salt

➊ Put the lemon grass in a food processor and add the ginger, garlic, onion, chillies, coriander, turmeric and cumin. Add the water and blend to a fairly fine paste.

➋ Blend in the caster sugar, fish sauce and lime juice, then turn the mixture into a bowl if you are not using it immediately. Cover and chill.

➌ Put the coconut milk into a heavy-based saucepan. Bring to the boil and cook for 10–15 minutes, until it has reduced by about a third and has thickened enough to coat a spoon very thinly.

➍ Tip the curry paste into the pan and whisk into the coconut milk. Reduce the heat to its lowest setting and cook the sauce very gently, covered, for 10 minutes. Season with salt and serve hot.

VEGETABLES
AND SALADS

Onion tarte tatin

Shallots are related to onions but form a cluster of small bulbs rather than a single one. They have a subtler flavour than onions and are not as pungent as garlic.

Preparation time 30 minutes, plus chilling
Cooking time 45–50 minutes
Serves 4–6

Pastry
175 g (6 oz) self-raising wholemeal flour
75 g (3 oz) chilled butter, diced
2 tablespoons chopped parsley
2 teaspoons chopped thyme
2–3 tablespoons lemon juice

Filling
500 g (1 lb) shallots, peeled
25 g (1 oz) butter
2 tablespoons olive oil
2 teaspoons muscovado sugar
salt and pepper

❶ Make the pastry. Sift the flour into a bowl and rub in the butter until the mixture resembles breadcrumbs. Stir in the herbs and lemon juice and mix to a firm dough. Knead briefly, then chill for 30 minutes.

❷ Make the filling. Boil the shallots for 10 minutes and drain well. Heat the butter and oil in an ovenproof frying pan and gently fry the shallots, stirring, for about 10 minutes until they start to colour. Sprinkle over the sugar, season to taste with salt and pepper and cook gently for 5 minutes until well coloured.

❸ Roll out the dough to a round, a little larger than the pan. Support the dough on the rolling pin and lay it over the shallots, tucking the edges of the pastry down the sides of the pan.

❹ Bake the tart in a preheated oven, 200°C (400°F), Gas Mark 6, for 20–25 minutes or until the pastry is crisp. Leave the tart to cool for 5 minutes, then put a large plate over the pan and invert the tart on to it. Serve warm or cold.

Roast vegetable and feta tart

Feta cheese, the best known Greek cheese, is made from ewes' milk. Its distinctive flavour goes well with these Mediterranean vegetables. Serve warm or cold.

Preparation time 25 minutes, plus chilling
Cooking time 45 minutes
Serves 6

Pastry
125 g (4 oz) self-raising flour
50 g (2 oz) oatmeal
75 g (3 oz) chilled butter, diced

Filling
1 aubergine, sliced
1 red pepper, cored, deseeded and cut into thick strips
1 onion, cut into wedges
2 courgettes, cut into thick slices
3 tomatoes, halved
2 garlic cloves, chopped
3 tablespoons olive oil
4 small sprigs of rosemary, plus extra for serving, if liked
125 g (4 oz) feta cheese, crumbled
2 tablespoons Parmesan cheese, grated
salt and pepper

1 Make the pastry. Mix together the flour and oatmeal then rub in the butter. Add 3 tablespoons cold water and mix to a firm dough. Knead briefly, then chill for 30 minutes.

2 Make the filling. Mix all the vegetables in a roasting tin. Add the garlic, oil and rosemary and season to taste.

3 Turn the mixture to coat the vegetables evenly and roast in a preheated oven, 200°C (400°F), Gas Mark 6, for 35 minutes.

4 Roll out the pastry and line a 23 cm (9 inch) dish. Bake blind (see page 44) for 15 minutes. Remove the paper and beans or foil and return to the oven for 5 minutes. Fill the pastry case with the vegetables, arrange the feta on top and sprinkle with Parmesan. Return to the oven for 10 minutes and serve garnished with extra rosemary, if liked.

Potato tart with ham, artichokes and mushrooms

This free-form tart has a moist, scone-like dough, which is perfect for all sorts of savoury toppings.

Preparation time 20 minutes
Cooking time 30–40 minutes
Serves 4

75 g (3 oz) butter
1 onion, thinly sliced
150 g (5 oz) plain flour
125 g (4 oz) mashed potato
1 tablespoon olive oil
2 shallots, sliced
125 g (4 oz) mushrooms, sliced
125 g (4 oz) cooked ham, cut into strips
175 g (6 oz) can artichoke hearts, drained and sliced
salt and pepper
sprigs of thyme, to garnish

1. Melt 25 g (1 oz) butter in a saucepan, add the onion and fry until it is softened and lightly browned. Leave to cool slightly. Dice the remaining butter and rub it into the flour in a bowl.

2. Add the onion with the pan juices and the mashed potato to the bowl and season to taste with salt and pepper. Mix to a soft dough.

3. Press out the dough on a prepared baking sheet to a 23 cm (9 inch) round. Pinch the edges of the dough to make a rim.

4. Heat the oil in a frying pan, add the shallots and fry until they are lightly browned. Add the mushrooms and cook briefly until softened.

5. Scatter the ham and artichokes over the dough, then top with the shallot and mushroom mixture. Season again if wished and bake in a preheated oven, 200°C (400°F), Gas Mark 6, for 25–30 minutes or until the pastry is golden-brown. Serve hot, garnished with thyme sprigs.

Butternut squash and Jarlsberg tart with oregano oil

Jarlsberg is a soft Norwegian cheese with a slightly nutty flavour. If you cannot find Jarlsberg, use Emmental instead.

Preparation time 20 minutes, plus chilling

Cooking time 1 hour

Serves 6

300 g (10 oz) shortcrust pastry (see page 46), thawed if frozen

1 tablespoon sun-dried tomato paste

1 kg (2 lb) butternut squash, peeled, halved and sliced; about 625 g (1¼ lb) prepared weight

250 g (8 oz) Jarlsberg cheese, rind removed and thinly sliced

2 tablespoons chopped oregano

3 tablespoons olive oil

6 thin slices Parma ham

1 Roll out the pastry on a lightly floured surface and line a 25 cm (10 inch) fluted tart tin. Spread the tomato paste over the base and chill for 30 minutes.

2 Arrange the slices of squash in the tart, overlapping each slice with the next. Push the slices of cheese between the slices of squash.

3 Stir the oregano into the oil and use half to brush over the tart. Bake the tart in a preheated oven, 180°C (350°F), Gas Mark 4, for 30 minutes. Remove from the oven.

4 Loosely arrange the slices of Parma ham over the tart, brush with the remaining herb oil and return to the oven for a further 30 minutes.

Dolcelatte and leek galette

Creamy blue dolcelatte has a smooth, mild flavour, which is ideal in rich sauces. Do not overcook the leeks, which can become tough and unpalatable.

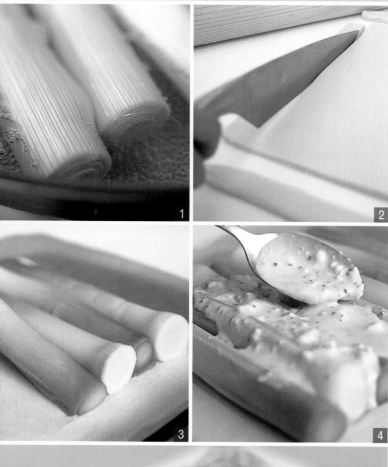

Preparation time 15 minutes
Cooking time 20–22 minutes
Serves 4

8 thin leeks
300 g (10 oz) puff pastry (see page 48), thawed if frozen
50 ml (2 fl oz) crème fraîche
1 teaspoon cayenne pepper
1 tablespoon wholegrain mustard
50 g (2 oz) dolcelatte cheese, crumbled
salt and pepper
chopped parsley, to garnish (optional)

❶ Trim the leeks to 20 cm (8 inches) and put them in a frying pan. Pour in enough boiling water to cover them and bring back to the boil. Reduce the heat, cover the pan and simmer for 5–7 minutes. Drain the leeks and set them aside.

❷ Roll out the pastry on a lightly floured surface to about 25 cm (10 inches) square and put it on a lightly oiled baking sheet. Use a sharp knife to score all the way round the pastry 3.5 cm (1¼ inches) in from the edge. Do not cut right through the pastry.

❸ Pat the leeks dry with kitchen paper to remove any excess moisture and arrange them on the pastry inside the border.

❹ Mix together the crème fraîche, cayenne, mustard and cheese and gently spread the mixture over the leeks. Season well with salt and pepper and cook in a preheated oven, 220°C (425°F), Gas Mark 7, for 15 minutes or until the pastry has risen and the border has browned.

❺ Cut the galette into quarters and sprinkle each portion with chopped parsley (if used). Serve immediately.

Roasted vegetables with orange and mustard glaze

A mixture of roasted root vegetables, such as carrots, parsnips, and turnips, makes a delicious alternative to roast potatoes.

Preparation time 20 minutes
Cooking time 1 hour 20 minutes
Serves 4

400 g (13 oz) carrots
400 g (13 oz) parsnips
300 g (10 oz) sweet potatoes
250 g (8 oz) small turnips
250 g (8 oz) shallots or baby onions, peeled and left whole
2 teaspoons finely chopped rosemary
6 tablespoons vegetable oil
4 teaspoons grainy mustard
finely grated rind of 1 orange, plus 3 tablespoons juice
1 tablespoon clear honey
1 tablespoon lemon juice
salt and pepper

1 Halve the carrots and parsnips lengthways and cut them into wedges. Cut the sweet potatoes into chunks. Peel and cut the turnips into wedges.

2 Bring a large saucepan of lightly salted water to the boil, tip in the prepared vegetables and cook for 5 minutes.

3 Drain well and transfer the vegetables to a large roasting tin. Scatter with the shallots or baby onions and sprinkle with the rosemary. Drizzle with the oil and toss together gently. Roast in a preheated oven, 200°C (400°F), Gas Mark 6, for 45 minutes until lightly browned.

4 Meanwhile, mix together the mustard, orange rind and juice, honey, lemon juice and a little seasoning. Drizzle over the vegetables and turn them until coated in the glaze.

5 Return to the oven and roast for a further 20–30 minutes, turning occasionally, until deep golden.

Panzanella

Ripe tomatoes and slightly stale country bread can be put to good use in this rustic Italian salad, which is ideal for lunch, a light supper or an appetizing starter.

Preparation time 15 minutes, plus standing

Cooking time 3–5 minutes

Serves 4

250 g (8 oz) ciabatta or country-style bread

100 ml (3½ fl oz) olive oil

500 g (1 lb) ripe tomatoes, skinned (see page 17)

½ small red onion, thinly sliced

handful of basil leaves, shredded

25 g (1 oz) anchovy fillets, drained and roughly chopped

2 tablespoons capers

1 garlic clove, crushed

2–3 tablespoons red wine vinegar

salt and pepper

1 Tear the bread into small pieces. Scatter them on a baking sheet and drizzle with 1 tablespoon oil. Grill until lightly browned.

2 Roughly chop the tomatoes and tip them into a salad bowl with any juices.

3 Add the onion, basil leaves, anchovies and capers to the salad bowl. Scatter with the bread.

4 Whisk the remaining oil with the garlic, 2 tablespoons vinegar and seasoning. (Add another tablespoon vinegar if you prefer a slightly tangier flavour.)

5 Drizzle the dressing over the salad and toss together lightly. Leave to stand for 20–30 minutes before serving.

Parsnip and potato rösti

These little potato cakes, made with grated potato, have a delicious texture. Sweet, young parsnips add lots of flavour for the perfect accompaniment to beef, lamb or game dishes.

Preparation time 15 minutes
Cooking time 15 minutes
Serves 4

500 g (1 lb) medium waxy potatoes
400 g (13 oz) small parsnips
2 garlic cloves, finely chopped
25 g (1 oz) butter
2–3 tablespoons olive oil
salt and pepper

1 Cut the potatoes and parsnips into large chunks. Bring a large saucepan of lightly salted water to the boil, add the potatoes and cook for 2 minutes. Add the parsnips and cook for a further 3 minutes. Drain and leave until cool enough to handle.

2 Coarsely grate the vegetables and mix together in a bowl. Sprinkle with the garlic and a little seasoning and mix together well.

3 Divide the mixture into 4 portions and pat each into a flat cake between the palms of your hands.

4 Melt the butter with 2 tablespoons oil in a large frying pan. Add the potato cakes and fry gently for about 5 minutes or until golden on the underside. Turn them over and fry for a further 5 minutes, drizzling with a little more oil if the pan is very dry.

Ratatouille

This Provençal vegetable stew can be served hot or cold and cooked to a firm or soft consistency, depending on preference. It also reheats well if you want to make it a day in advance.

Preparation time 25 minutes

Cooking time 30 minutes

Serves 6

150 ml (¼ pint) olive oil

1 kg (2 lb) well-flavoured tomatoes

½ teaspoon caster sugar

2 teaspoons chopped rosemary or thyme

2 onions, thinly sliced

3 red or yellow peppers, or a mixture of the two, deseeded and cut into small chunks

1 large aubergine, about 400 g (13 oz), halved lengthways and thinly sliced

2 courgettes, sliced

3 garlic cloves, chopped

salt and pepper

1 Skin the tomatoes following the instructions on page 17. Chop the flesh roughly.

2 Heat half the oil in a saucepan, add the tomatoes, sugar, herbs and a little seasoning and fry gently, stirring frequently, for about 10 minutes or until the tomatoes are soft. Raise the temperature and cook quickly for about 5 minutes until the mixture has thickened.

3 In a separate, large saucepan or frying pan, fry the onions in the remaining oil for about 5 minutes or until softened. Add the peppers and aubergines and fry gently, stirring for 5 minutes. Stir in the courgettes and garlic and fry for a further 5 minutes.

4 Combine the two mixtures, using whichever pan is the larger. Cook gently for about 15 minutes or until the vegetables are tender but retain a little texture. Check the seasoning and serve.

Fig, gorgonzola and Parma ham salad

This pasta salad combines sweet and salty flavours, tossed in a honey and orange dressing. The figs must be sweet, ripe and juicy.

Preparation time 10 minutes

Cooking time 2–10 minutes

Serves 4–6

200 g (7 oz) fresh or dried pappardelle

2 tablespoons clear honey

2 teaspoons coarse grain mustard

3 tablespoons freshly squeezed orange juice

squeeze of lemon juice

3 tablespoons mild olive oil

4 ripe, juicy figs, cut into thin wedges

100 g (3½ oz) Parma ham, torn into small pieces

150 g (5 oz) Gorgonzola cheese, roughly diced

salt and pepper

❶ Bring a large saucepan of lightly salted water to the boil. Add the pasta, return to the boil and cook, allowing 2–3 minutes for fresh and 8–10 minutes for dried.

❷ Meanwhile, whisk together the honey, mustard, orange and lemon juice, oil and a little salt and pepper.

❸ Drain the pasta and return it to the saucepan.

❹ Gently mix the figs, ham and Gorgonzola into the pasta and transfer to serving plates. Spoon over the dressing and serve.

Chicken, mangetout and peach salad

This salad is a delicious concoction of complimentary colours and flavours, from sweet and juicy peaches to the saltiness of the dressing.

Preparation time 15 minutes
Cooking time 10 minutes
Serves 4

200 g (7 oz) dried pasta shapes, such as rigatoni, lumaconi or trompretti

125 g (4 oz) mangetout, sliced diagonally

2 large, juicy peaches

200 g (7 oz) lean, cooked chicken, roughly sliced

½ bunch of spring onions, sliced diagonally

15 g (½ oz) coriander leaves, chopped

salt and pepper

Dressing

3 tablespoons clear honey

3 tablespoons lemon juice

4 tablespoons mild olive oil

1 tablespoon soy sauce

2 teaspoons Thai fish sauce

① Bring a large saucepan of lightly salted water to the boil, add the pasta and cook for 8–10 minutes until just tender. Add the mangetout and cook for a further minute. Drain and rinse under cold running water. Drain thoroughly and turn into a large bowl.

② Halve, stone and thinly slice the peaches and add them to the bowl with the chicken, spring onions and coriander.

③ Make the dressing by whisking together the honey, lemon juice, olive oil, soy sauce and fish sauce.

④ Just before serving, pour the dressing over the salad, season with pepper and toss the ingredients together well.

Spicy lentil and halloumi salad

Salty halloumi cheese and a sweet and tangy dressed lentil salad make a delicious balance of flavours. The salad can be served warm, freshly prepared, but is also good served chilled.

Preparation time 15 minutes

Cooking time 25 minutes

Serves 4

225 g (7½ oz) puy lentils

1 tablespoon vegetable bouillon powder

3 bay leaves

1 onion, halved

225 g (7½ oz) halloumi cheese

100 ml (3½ fl oz) olive oil

2 teaspoons coriander seeds

2 teaspoons cumin seeds

1 bunch of spring onions, thinly sliced

finely grated rind of 1 lemon, plus 4 tablespoons juice

2 tablespoons clear honey

2 celery sticks, very thinly sliced

4 tablespoons chopped coriander

pepper

① Rinse the lentils and put them in a saucepan with the bouillon powder, bay leaves and onion and cover with plenty of cold water. Bring to the boil, reduce the heat and simmer gently for 20 minutes until the lentils are tender. Drain, discarding the onion but leaving the bay leaves, and tip the lentils into a bowl.

② Pat the cheese between several sheets of kitchen paper to remove the moisture. Cut the cheese into small chunks. Heat 1 tablespoon oil in a frying pan and fry the cheese on all sides until the pieces begin to brown.

③ Crush the seeds in a pestle and mortar. Tip them into a small saucepan and add the remaining oil and the spring onions. Heat gently for 30 seconds to infuse the flavours together. Remove from the heat and add the lemon rind and juice and honey. Season with plenty of pepper.

④ Pour the dressing over the lentils and add the celery, coriander and cheese. Toss the ingredients together and serve warm or cold.

Sardine salad with herb and caper dressing

As lovely as plain grilled or barbecued sardines are, it's good to be experimental with them now and again. This fresh, clean-tasting salad makes an appetizing summer starter – or a light meal for two.

Preparation time 20 minutes
Cooking time 50 minutes
Serves 4

400 g (13 oz) young raw beetroot
6 tablespoons extra virgin olive oil
500 g (1 lb) sardines, gutted, with heads and tails removed
1 small garlic clove, finely chopped
1 tablespoon lemon juice
1 teaspoon finely chopped rosemary
2 tablespoons capers, rinsed and drained
50 g (2 oz) rocket or herb salad
125 g (4 oz) mild goats' cheese
salt and pepper

1. Trim and scrub the beetroot, then cut into small wedges. Put the pieces in a small roasting tin and toss with 1 tablespoon oil. Roast in a preheated oven, 200°C (400°F), Gas Mark 6, for 40 minutes or until just tender.

2. Add the sardines to the tin and drizzle with another 1 tablespoon oil. Roast for a further 10 minutes or until the sardines are cooked through.

3. Whisk together the remaining oil with the garlic, lemon juice, rosemary, capers and salt and pepper to taste.

4. Cut the sardines along the backbones and lift the fillets from the bones.

5. Put the salad leaves on serving plates and arrange the beetroot and sardines on top. Crumble or chop the goats' cheese and scatter it over the top. Spoon over the dressing and serve.

Gribiche sauce

Like mayonnaise, gribiche is made by gradually working oil into eggs. It is delicious with hot or cold vegetables, particularly asparagus. The egg yolk paste can be made in advance.

Preparation time 15 minutes
Serves 4

4 hard-boiled egg yolks
1 teaspoon Dijon mustard
200 ml (7 fl oz) light olive oil
1–2 tablespoons white wine vinegar
2 tablespoons capers, rinsed and roughly chopped
2 tablespoons chives, snipped
white of 1 hard-boiled egg, chopped (optional)
salt and pepper
extra snipped chives or chive flowers, to garnish

1 Pound together the egg yolks, mustard and a little salt and pepper using a large pestle and mortar. Alternatively, put the ingredients into a food processor or blender and mix together lightly.

2 Drizzle in a little of the oil, mixing well until blended. Keep drizzling in more oil until you have incorporated about half and the mixture makes a thick paste. Add 1 tablespoon wine vinegar. Gradually blend in the remaining oil. (Don't add the oil too quickly or the sauce might separate.)

3 Turn the sauce into a bowl or jug and stir in the capers and chives.

4 Add a little more wine vinegar and salt and pepper if necessary.

5 Spoon the sauce over vegetables and sprinkle with the egg white (if used) and garnish with chives or chive flowers.

Hot harissa sauce

This is a quick and easy sauce with plenty of flavour. Use the entire mixture to stir into sautéed vegetables and beans, as a wonderful couscous topping or to accompany roast tomatoes.

Preparation time 10 minutes, plus chilling
Cooking time 5 minutes
Serves 4–6

1 tablespoon coriander seeds
1 teaspoon caraway seeds
3 tablespoons light olive oil
1 red pepper, deseeded and roughly chopped
1 small red onion, roughly chopped
1 red chilli, deseeded and chopped
3 garlic cloves, chopped
4 tablespoons coriander leaves, torn into pieces
½ teaspoon celery salt
150 ml (5 oz) passata

❶ Use a pestle and mortar to grind the coriander and caraway seeds until lightly crushed. Alternatively, use a small bowl and the end of a rolling pin.

❷ Tip the seeds into a small frying pan and add the oil, red pepper and onion. Cook gently for 5 minutes or until the vegetables are soft.

❸ Transfer the cooked mixture to a food processor or blender and add the chilli, garlic, coriander, celery salt and passata.

❹ Blend until smooth, scraping the mixture down from the sides of the bowl if necessary. Transfer to a serving bowl and cover with clingfilm. Chill until ready to serve. The sauce will keep well in the refrigerator, tightly wrapped, for up to 5 days.

Griddled aubergine sauce

This unusual sauce is mildly spiced without being overpowering. For a hotter flavour, add a finely chopped red or green chilli. Char the aubergines well to give the sauce a rich colour and flavour.

Preparation time 15 minutes
Cooking time 30 minutes
Serves 6–8

½ teaspoon celery salt

1 teaspoon mild chilli powder

400 g (13 oz) aubergines, sliced lengthways

6 tablespoons sunflower oil

1 large red onion, chopped

3 garlic cloves, chopped

1 tablespoon black onion seeds

1 teaspoon ground fenugreek

6–8 large mint leaves, chopped

150 ml (¼ pint) Vegetable Stock (see page 19)

3 tablespoons sun-dried tomato paste

100 ml (3½ fl oz) crème fraîche

❶ Mix together the celery salt and chilli powder and rub the mixture over the aubergine slices. Brush one side of each slice with a little oil. Lay several slices, oiled sides down, on a preheated griddle. Cook the aubergine slices, in batches, until charred, which will take about 6 minutes. Turn them over, brush with more oil and cook until soft.

❷ Heat the remaining oil in a large frying pan, add the onion and garlic and fry gently for 3 minutes. Add the onion seeds, fenugreek and mint and fry for a further 2 minutes.

❸ Tip the onion mixture into a food processor or blender. Add the aubergine slices and blend to a slightly chunky paste.

❹ Turn the mixture into a clean pan and add the stock and tomato paste. Heat through gently, stirring, swirl in the crème fraîche and serve.

Green tomato chutney

If you grow tomatoes you will probably be left with some unripened fruit at the end of the season. But don't throw green tomatoes away: chop them up and make a tempting chutney.

Preparation time 15 minutes
Cooking time 1 hour 40 minutes
Makes about 2 kg (4 lb)

1 kg (2 lb) green tomatoes, finely chopped
500 g (1 lb) onions, finely chopped
500 g (1 lb) cooking apples, peeled, cored and chopped
2 fresh green chillies, halved, deseeded and finely chopped
2 garlic cloves, crushed
1 teaspoon ground ginger
generous pinch of ground cloves
generous pinch of ground turmeric
50 g (2 oz) raisins
250 g (8 oz) soft dark brown sugar
300 ml (½ pint) white wine vinegar

1 Put the tomatoes, onions, apples and chillies into a large, heavy-based pan and mix together.

2 Add the garlic, ginger, cloves and turmeric, then stir in the raisins, sugar and vinegar.

3 Bring to the boil, reduce the heat and cover the pan. Simmer, stirring frequently, for 1¼–1½ hours or until the chutney has thickened.

4 Transfer the chutney to warm, dry jars and cover the surface of each with a disc of waxed paper, waxed side down, then top with an airtight lid. Label and leave the chutney to mature in a cool, dark place for at least 3 weeks before using, or store, unopened, for 6–12 months.

Chestnut, red onion and fennel chutney

This chutney is quick and easy to prepare and is the perfect partner to blue cheese, bread and cold meats for a quick and delicious lunch.

Preparation time 15 minutes
Cooking time 1½ hours
Makes about 625 g (1¼ lb)

60 ml (2½ fl oz) olive oil
4 large red onions, thinly sliced
1 fennel bulb, trimmed and thinly sliced
250 g (8 oz) cooked, peeled chestnuts, halved
100 g (3½ oz) soft light brown sugar
125 ml (4 fl oz) cider vinegar
125 ml (4 fl oz) sweet sherry or Marsala
pepper

1 Heat the oil in a large, heavy-based pan, add the onions and fennel and cook gently for 25–30 minutes or until the onions are very soft.

2 Add the chestnuts, sugar, vinegar and sherry or Marsala to the pan, season well with pepper and stir.

3 Simmer gently, uncovered, stirring occasionally, for about 1 hour or until the chutney has thickened.

4 Transfer the chutney to warm, dry jars and cover the surface of each with a disc of waxed paper, waxed side down, then top with an airtight lid. Label and leave to cool completely before serving. Store in a cool, dark place or in the refrigerator. It will keep, unopened, for 3–4 months.

Beetroot and apple relish

Relishes, as their name suggests, are spicy and particularly suitable for serving with grills and barbecues. The beetroot in this recipe gives this relish a wonderful fresh taste.

Preparation time 15 minutes
Cooking time 1¾ hours
Makes about 1.5 kg (3 lb)

500 g (1 lb) cooking apples, peeled, halved and cored
500 g (1 lb) raw beetroot, peeled
375 g (12 oz) onions, finely chopped
1 tablespoon finely chopped fresh root ginger
2 large garlic cloves, crushed
1 teaspoon paprika
1 teaspoon ground turmeric
1 cinnamon stick
250 g (8 oz) soft dark brown sugar
450 ml (¾ pint) red wine vinegar

❶ Grate the apples and beetroot into a large, heavy-based pan.

❷ Add the onion, ginger and garlic to the pan and stir to combine with the beetroot and apple.

❸ Add the remaining ingredients and bring the mixture to the boil, then reduce the heat and cover the pan. Simmer, stirring occasionally, for about 1½ hours, until the relish has thickened and the beetroot is tender.

❹ Transfer the relish to warm, dry jars and top with airtight lids. Label and leave to mature in a cool, dark place for about 1 week before using, or store, unopened, for 6–9 months.

Tomato ketchup

Homemade ketchups are spiced fruit or vegetable purées that can be delicate or pronounced in flavour. Serve in the traditional way with chips and grilled meats.

Preparation time 15 minutes
Cooking time 1 hour
Makes about 1.2 litres (2 pints)

1.5 kg (3 lb) ripe, well-flavoured tomatoes, roughly chopped
500 g (1 lb) onions, roughly chopped
125 g (4 oz) sugar
3 tablespoons mustard powder
3 garlic cloves, crushed
1 teaspoon salt
150 ml (¼ pint) red wine vinegar

1 Put all the ingredients into a large, heavy-based saucepan and mix well. Bring the mixture to the boil, then reduce the heat and simmer, uncovered, stirring occasionally, for 45 minutes.

2 Allow the ketchup to cool slightly, then blend to a purée in a food processor or blender.

3 Press the purée through a sieve and transfer the smooth sauce to a clean pan.

4 Bring the ketchup back to boiling point, then take the pan off the heat. Transfer the ketchup to warm, dry bottles or jars and seal with airtight tops. Label and leave to cool, then store in a cool, dark place. It will keep for up to 6 months.

FISH
AND SEAFOOD

Devilled oysters

This is a good recipe to try if you baulk at the idea of eating raw oysters. When you buy them, try to get an oyster knife, which makes the task of shucking the oysters much easier.

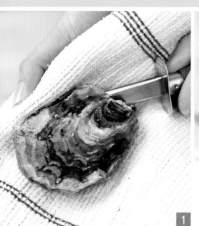   

Preparation time 25 minutes
Cooking time 15 minutes
Serves 4

12 oysters

1 teaspoon mustard seeds

75 g (3 oz) butter

2 shallots, finely chopped

½ celery stick, finely chopped

1 garlic clove, crushed

1 tablespoon white wine vinegar

1 teaspoon Tabasco sauce

1 tablespoon chopped chives

1 tablespoon chopped flat leaf parsley

plenty of sea or rock salt and pepper

❶ To shuck the oysters, hold an oyster, wrapped in a thick cloth, with the rounded shell underneath. Push a strong knife, preferably an oyster knife, into the small gap at the hinged end. Twist the knife to sever the muscle and separate the shells.

❷ Discard the top shell. Run the blade of the knife under the oyster to loosen it, holding the shell steady to prevent the juices from running out. Place the oyster in a grill pan, lined with a layer of salt to keep the shells from flopping over. Repeat with the remainder.

❸ Dry-fry the mustard seeds in a nonstick frying pan until they start to pop. Add the butter, shallots and celery and fry for 3 minutes. Add the garlic and a little seasoning and fry for a further 2 minutes. Stir in the vinegar, Tabasco sauce and two-thirds of each herb.

❹ Spoon the mixture over the oysters and cook under a preheated grill for 5–8 minutes or until the oysters are just firm. Serve scattered with the remaining herbs.

Frazzled squid and pasta

Cooling cucumber, crispy fried squid and fresh herbs make this dish visually stunning and full of flavour. Serve with a large pasta shape, such as rigatoni.

Preparation time 25 minutes

Cooking time 15 minutes

Serves 4–6

½ cucumber, peeled and sliced

1 tablespoon salt, plus extra for cooking

200 g (3½ oz) dried pasta shapes

100 g (5 oz) rocket

100 ml (3½ fl oz) olive oil

500 g (1 lb) cleaned small squid

1 teaspoon ground paprika

1 tablespoon plain flour

1–2 tablespoons lemon juice

1 teaspoon caster sugar

40 g (1½ oz) mixed herbs, such as parsley, chives, basil and fennel

pepper

❶ Layer the cucumber in a small colander, sprinkling each layer lightly with the salt.

❷ Bring a large saucepan of lightly salted water to the boil. Add the pasta, return to the boil and cook for 10 minutes or until just tender. Drain and tip into a bowl. Add the rocket and 1 tablespoon oil and toss the ingredients together.

❸ Rinse the squid, halve lengthways and pat dry on kitchen paper. (If the tentacles are present cut them from the heads and use them as well.)

❹ Toss the paprika with the flour and coat the squid. Heat another 2 tablespoons oil and fry the squid for 4–5 minutes until golden. Drain.

❺ Put the remaining oil in a blender with 1 tablespoon lemon juice, the sugar, herbs and pepper. Blend until finely chopped. Rinse the cucumber in several changes of cold water to remove the salt and drain. Add to the pasta with the squid and dressing. Mix together and drizzle with a little extra lemon juice, if needed.

Dill-pickled salmon

In this well-loved Scandinavian dish, salmon is pickled in a delicious, sweet dill marinade. Allow two or three days for making the salmon and serve with rye or granary bread.

Preparation time 20 minutes, plus marinating
Serves 8–10

2 middle-cut salmon fillets, each about 500 g (1 lb), scaled and boned
25 g (1 oz) chopped dill
40 g (1½ oz) coarse sea salt
50 g (2 oz) caster sugar
2 tablespoons black peppercorns, crushed

Sauce
2 tablespoons French brown mustard
4 teaspoons caster sugar
4 tablespoons chopped dill
100 ml (3½ fl oz) Mayonnaise (see page 21)

1 Lay one salmon fillet, skin side down, in a shallow, non-metallic dish. Mix together the dill, salt, sugar and peppercorns and scatter the mixture over the fish. Cover with the second piece of fish, skin side up.

2 Cover the dish with foil, place a small tray or plate over it and balance several kitchen weights or full cans on top.

3 Chill for 2–3 days, turning the fish over once or twice a day and spooning the juices that seep out over the fish.

4 Drain each salmon fillet and put on to a chopping board. Using a very sharp knife, cut off thin, slanting slices, not much thicker than smoked salmon.

5 Make the sauce by beating together all the ingredients. Put the mixture in a small serving dish and serve with the salmon.

Escabèche

There are many variations on the theme of steeping lightly cooked fish in seasoned, sweetened vinegar. This delicious version is made with succulent pieces of chunky cod.

Preparation time 15 minutes, plus chilling
Cooking time 10 minutes
Serves 4

500 g (1 lb) cod fillet, skinned
4 tablespoons olive oil
1 pointed red pepper, deseeded and thinly sliced
1 red onion, thinly sliced
2 pared strips of orange rind, plus 2 tablespoons juice
½ teaspoon cumin seeds, crushed
good pinch of ground turmeric
125 ml (4 fl oz) sherry vinegar
5 tablespoons light muscovado sugar
8 pitted green olives
salt and pepper

❶ Cut the cod into chunky pieces, discarding any stray bones, and season lightly with salt and pepper.

❷ Heat the oil in a frying pan and gently fry the fish on both sides for about 5 minutes or until just cooked through. Drain to a non-metallic dish in which the pieces fit quite snugly. Gently fry the red pepper and onion in the pan until softened and add them to the dish. Tuck the orange rind between the pieces of fish.

❸ Mix together the orange juice, cumin seeds, turmeric, vinegar and sugar until the sugar has dissolved.

❹ Pour the mixture over the fish. Turn the ingredients gently to combine. Cover and chill for up to 3 days. Serve scattered with the olives.

Roasted mackerel with sweet potatoes

Chilli-infused olive oil adds a hot spiciness that's lovely with the cooling mint raita and sweet caramelized potatoes and onions. Alternatively, use mild olive oil and a thinly sliced red chilli.

Preparation time 15 minutes
Cooking time 1 hour
Serves 2

375 g (12 oz) sweet potatoes
1 red onion, thinly sliced
4 tablespoons chilli-infused olive oil
several sprigs of thyme
40 g (1½ oz) sun-dried tomatoes, thinly sliced
4 large mackerel fillets
salt and pepper
lemon wedges, to serve

Raita
100 ml (3½ fl oz) natural yogurt
1 tablespoon chopped coriander
1 tablespoon chopped mint

1 Scrub the sweet potatoes and cut them into 1.5 cm (¾ inch) chunks. Scatter the pieces in a shallow, ovenproof dish with the onion. Add the oil, thyme and a little salt and mix together.

2 Bake in a preheated oven, 200°C (400°F), Gas Mark 6, for 40–45 minutes, turning once or twice, until the potatoes are just tender and beginning to brown. Stir in the tomatoes.

3 Fold each mackerel fillet in half, skin side out, and place on top of the potatoes. Return to the oven for a further 12–15 minutes or until the fish is cooked through and tender.

4 Meanwhile, mix together the yogurt, herbs and a little seasoning in a serving bowl.

5 Transfer the fish and potatoes to warm serving plates, spoon over the raita or place in a bowl for dipping. Serve with lemon wedges.

Seafood paella

The secret of a good paella is to sauté the ingredients in the oil before you cook the rice so that the oil carries plenty of flavour. You can substitute other fish and shellfish as you wish.

Preparation time 30 minutes

Cooking time 40 minutes

Serves 4

150 ml (¼ pint) olive oil

350 g (11½ oz) cleaned squid, sliced into rings if large (see page 39)

8 large raw prawns, peeled and deveined

2 red or green peppers, deseeded and sliced

125 g (4 oz) piece chorizo sausage, diced

4 garlic cloves, crushed

1 onion, chopped

250 g (8 oz) paella rice

450 ml (¾ pint) Fish Stock (see page 19)

1 teaspoon saffron strands

100 g (3½ oz) peas

300–400 g (10–13 oz) mussels, cleaned (see page 39)

salt and pepper

lemon wedges, to serve

1 Heat half the oil in a large paella or frying pan and fry the squid and prawns, stirring, for 5 minutes. Drain with a slotted spoon. Add the peppers and fry for a further 5 minutes. Drain.

2 Add the chorizo, garlic, onion and remaining oil to the pan and fry for 5 minutes.

3 Sprinkle in the rice and cook for 1 minute, stirring so that the grains become coated in the spicy oil.

4 Stir in the stock and saffron and bring to the boil. Reduce the heat, cover with a lid or foil and cook gently for about 20 minutes or until the rice is cooked through. Stir in the peas, along with the squid, prawns and peppers.

5 Push the mussels into the rice so that they are half submerged. Cover and cook for 3–4 minutes or until the mussels have opened. Discard any that remain closed. Season and serve with lemon wedges.

Parchment-baked fish

Sealing portions of fish in their own little parcels is a brilliant way of trapping in all the flavour and moisture. You could try serving mini parcels for starter-sized portions.

Preparation time 20 minutes
Cooking time 20 minutes
Serves 4

2 tablespoons sesame oil, plus extra for brushing
4 shark or swordfish fillets, each about 200 g (7 oz), skinned
75 g (3 oz) shiitake mushrooms, sliced
50 g (2 oz) sugar snap peas, halved lengthways
1 mild red chilli, thinly sliced
40 g (1½ oz) fresh root ginger, grated
2 garlic cloves, crushed

Dressing
2 tablespoons light soy sauce
2 tablespoons lime juice
2 tablespoons sweet chilli sauce
4 tablespoons chopped fresh coriander

❶ Cut out 4 squares, each 30 x 30 cm (12 x 12 inches), of baking parchment and brush the centres of each with a little sesame oil. Place a piece of fish in the centre of each square. Mix together the mushrooms, sugar snap peas and chilli and pile the mixture on top of the fish.

❷ Mix together the sesame oil, ginger and garlic and spoon over the vegetables. Bring the sides of the parchment up over the fish as though wrapping a parcel. Fold the edges together and flatten gently.

❸ Flatten the ends and fold them over to seal. Place the parcels on a baking sheet and bake in a preheated oven, 190°C (375°F), Gas Mark 5, for 20 minutes. Open one of the parcels and test whether the fish is cooked through. If necessary return to the oven for a few more minutes.

❹ Meanwhile, make the dressing by mixing together the soy sauce, lime juice, chilli sauce and coriander. Loosen the parcels and spoon the dressing over the fish before serving.

Portuguese fish stew

You can use almost any white fish in this flexible stew, so take your pick of the freshest and best on offer. Serve with crusty bread for dipping in the delicious juices.

Preparation time 25 minutes

Cooking time 45 minutes

Serves 6

400 g (13 oz) cleaned small squid (see page 39)

1.5 kg (3 lb) mixed white fish, such as hake, haddock or monkfish fillet, red mullet, shark or swordfish

6 tablespoons olive oil

2 onions, chopped

3 green peppers, deseeded and quartered

4 garlic cloves, finely chopped

750 g (1½ lb) tomatoes, skinned (see page 17) and chopped

800 g (1 lb 10 oz) floury potatoes, cut into chunks

1 glass dry white wine

600 ml (1 pint) Fish Stock (see page 19)

4 tablespoons sun-dried tomato paste

3 bay leaves

25 g (1 oz) chopped fresh coriander

salt and pepper

① Slice the squid if more than about 5 cm (2 inches) long and reserve the tentacles, if liked.

② Cut the fish into large chunks, discarding the skin and any bones. (If you are using red mullet, there is no need to remove the skin from the fish.)

③ Heat half the oil in a large, heavy-based saucepan and gently fry the onions and green peppers until softened. Add the garlic, tomatoes, potatoes, wine, stock, tomato paste, bay leaves and remaining oil and simmer, uncovered, for 30 minutes.

④ Lower the white fish into the stew and cook gently for 5 minutes. Add the squid and coriander and cook for a further 5 minutes or until all the fish is cooked through. Season to taste and serve in large, shallow bowls with hunks of crusty bread.

Tuna polpettes

Made using either minced meat or fish, polpettes are a
Mediterranean version of a burger. This recipe uses fresh tuna,
but can be made equally well with swordfish or shark.

Preparation time 30 minutes
Cooking time 1 hour 25 minutes
Serves 4

1 quantity Roasted Tomato Sauce (see page 23)
25 g (1 oz) bread
2 tablespoons milk
3 tablespoons olive oil
1 small red onion, finely chopped
500 g (1 lb) fresh tuna, cut into chunks
150 g (5 oz) mozzarella cheese
1 tablespoon finely chopped oregano
salt and pepper

❶ Make the Roasted Tomato Sauce. Break the bread into
pieces and soak in a bowl with the milk until soft.
Mash to a pulp. Heat 1 tablespoon oil in a frying pan
and fry the onion until softened. Push the tuna through
a mincer or briefly use a food processor to mince
the fish, taking care not to mince it to a purée. Mix
together the tuna, onion, bread and a little seasoning.

❷ Divide the mixture into 8 equal portions. Roll each into
a ball and flatten into little burger shapes.

❸ Heat the remaining oil in the frying pan and fry the
polpettes on both sides to brown. Tip half the tomato
sauce into a shallow, ovenproof dish and arrange the
polpettes over the sauce.

❹ Cut the mozzarella into 8 thin slices and arrange them
over the polpettes. Scatter with the oregano and
seasoning and bake in a preheated oven, 180°C (350°F),
Gas Mark 4, for 20–25 minutes or until heated through.
Meanwhile, reheat the remaining sauce to serve.

Prawn and courgette tart

Use a young, firm courgette with a dark green, glossy skin. As they age, the skins of courgettes become duller and the flavour is less intense.

Preparation time 25 minutes, plus chilling
Cooking time 40 minutes
Serves 4–6

175 g (6 oz) shortcrust pastry (see page 46), thawed if frozen
40 g (1½ oz) butter
1 courgette, cut into matchsticks
25 g (1 oz) plain flour
300 ml (½ pint) hot milk
175 g (6 oz) peeled cooked prawns, thawed if frozen
2 eggs, beaten
75 g (3 oz) mature Cheddar cheese, grated
salt and pepper

❶ Roll out the pastry on a lightly floured surface and line a 23 cm (9 inch) tart tin. Chill for 30 minutes, then bake the pastry case blind (see page 46) in a preheated oven, 200°C (400°F), Gas Mark 6, for 15 minutes. Remove the paper and beans or foil. Reduce the oven temperature to 190°C (375°F), Gas Mark 5. Meanwhile, make the filling. Melt the butter in a saucepan, add the courgette matchsticks and cook gently for about 5 minutes or until softened.

❷ Stir in the flour and cook for 1 minute. Gradually stir in the hot milk, cooking until the sauce is thick and smooth.

❸ Let the sauce cool slightly, then stir in the prawns, eggs and 50 g (2 oz) cheese. Season to taste with salt and pepper.

❹ Pour the filling into the pastry case and sprinkle with the remaining grated cheese.

❺ Bake the tart in a preheated oven for about 25 minutes or until the filling is golden-brown. Serve warm.

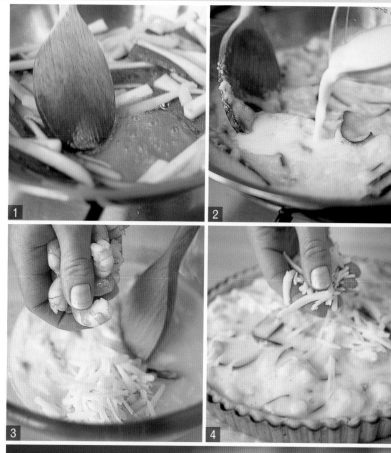

Sea bream in a salt crust

This Spanish cooking technique is one of the best ways to enjoy absolutely fresh fish. Sea bass or snapper are really good or, if you can get one, a small turbot.

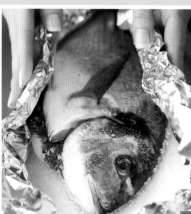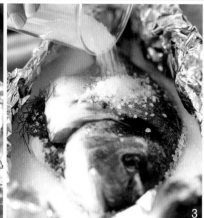

Preparation time 15 minutes

Cooking time 25 minutes

Serves 4

1.75 kg (3½ lb) coarse sea salt

1.25–1.5 kg (2½–3 lb) sea bream

small bunch of herbs, such as thyme, parsley and fennel, plus extra to serve

1 lemon, sliced

pepper

To serve

Aïoli

lemon wedges

❶ Use foil to line a roasting tin that is large enough to hold the whole fish and scatter the base with a thin layer of salt. Rinse the fish but do not dry it and place it on top of the salt, diagonally if necessary. Tuck the herbs and lemon slices into the cavity and season with black pepper.

❷ Pull up the foil around the fish so that there is a lining of salt about 1.5 cm (¾ inch) thick around the fish.

❸ Scatter the fish with an even covering of salt about 1 cm (½ inch) thick. Drizzle or spray the salt with a little water and bake in a preheated oven, 200°C (400°F), Gas Mark 6, for 25 minutes. To check that the fish is cooked, pierce a metal skewer into the thickest part of the fish and leave for a few seconds before removing. If the skewer is very hot, the fish is cooked through.

❹ Lift away the salt crust and peel away the skin. Serve the fish in chunky pieces and then lift away the central bone and head so that you can serve the bottom fillet. Serve with lemon wedges, aïoli and herbs.

Oven-steamed salmon with Asian greens

Oven-steaming fish is pretty effortless – just make sure that
the rack sits at least 1 cm (½ inch) above the base of the tin.

Preparation time 15 minutes
Cooking time 25 minutes
Serves 4

4 chunky salmon steaks, each about 200 g (7 oz)
1 tablespoon tamarind paste
2–3 tablespoons soy sauce
15 g (½ oz) fresh root ginger, peeled and grated
2 teaspoons caster sugar
2 garlic cloves, crushed
1 mild green chilli, finely sliced
1 teaspoon cornflour
250 g (8 oz) pak choi
8 spring onions, halved lengthways
15 g (½ oz) fresh coriander, chopped

1 Put the salmon steaks on an oiled roasting rack
or wire rack inside a roasting tin and pour 450 ml
(¾ pint) boiling water into the tin. Cover tightly with
foil and cook in a preheated oven, 180°C (350°F), Gas
Mark 4, for 15 minutes or until the salmon is almost
cooked through.

2 Meanwhile, put the tamarind in a small saucepan and
blend in 175 ml (6 fl oz) water. Stir in the soy sauce,
ginger, sugar, garlic and chilli and heat through gently
for 5 minutes. Blend the cornflour with 1 tablespoon
water and add to the pan. Heat gently, stirring, for
1–2 minutes or until thickened.

3 Quarter the pak choi lengthways into wedges and
arrange the pieces around the salmon on the rack
with the spring onions. Re-cover and return to the
oven for a further 8–10 minutes or until the vegetables
have wilted.

4 Stir the coriander into the sauce. Transfer the fish and
greens to warm plates and serve with the sauce.

Moroccan fish tagine

This spicy, aromatic stew can be made using chunky fillets of almost any white fish. For best results, the pieces need to be large so that they don't disintegrate during the slow cooking.

Preparation time 15 minutes

Cooking time 55 minutes

Serves 4

750 g (1½ lb) firm white fish fillets, such as cod, sea bass or monkfish, skinned

½ teaspoon cumin seeds

½ teaspoon coriander seeds

6 cardamom pods

4 tablespoons olive oil

2 small onions, thinly sliced

2 garlic cloves, crushed

¼ teaspoon ground turmeric

1 cinnamon stick

40 g (1½ oz) sultanas

25 g (1 oz) pine nuts, lightly toasted

150 ml (¼ pint) Fish Stock (see page 19)

finely grated rind of 1 lemon, plus 1 tablespoon juice

salt and pepper

chopped parsley, to garnish

❶ Cut the fish into large chunks, each about 5 cm (2 inches) square, and season.

❷ Use a pestle and mortar to crush the cumin and coriander seeds and cardamom pods. Discard the cardamom pods, leaving the seeds.

❸ Heat the oil in a large, shallow frying pan and gently fry the onions for 6–8 minutes until golden. Add the garlic and the spices and fry gently, stirring, for 2 minutes. Add the fish pieces, turning them until they are coated in the oil. Transfer the fish and onions to an ovenproof casserole dish and scatter with the sultanas and pine nuts.

❹ Add the stock and lemon rind and juice to the frying pan and bring to the boil. Pour the mixture around the fish, cover with a lid and bake in a preheated oven, 160°C (325°F), Gas Mark 3, for 40 minutes.

Tuna Wellington

A good-sized piece of tuna, about 20 x 8.5 cm (8 x 3½ inches), is ideal for this dish. If you buy a fillet that's very chunky at one end, trim off the excess and grill or fry it for flaking into salads.

Preparation time 30 minutes, plus cooling
Cooking time 40 minutes
Serves 6

1 kg (2 lb) piece fresh tuna
50 g (2 oz) butter
1 shallot, finely chopped
350 g (11½ oz) mushrooms, roughly chopped
2 tablespoons hot horseradish sauce
3 tablespoons chopped tarragon
400 g (13 oz) puff pastry (see page 48), thawed if frozen
beaten egg, to glaze
salt and pepper

❶ Pat the tuna dry on kitchen paper and rub all over with salt and pepper. Melt a knob of the butter in a frying pan and sear the tuna on all sides until browned. Drain and leave to cool.

❷ Add half the remaining butter to the pan and gently fry the shallot and mushrooms until browned and all the moisture has evaporated. Stir in the horseradish sauce and tarragon and leave to cool. Spread the remaining butter over the tuna.

❸ Roll out the pastry on a lightly floured surface to a large rectangle. Press half the mushroom mixture over the top of the tuna with your hands. Invert on to the pastry and spread with the remaining mushroom mixture.

❹ Brush the pastry with beaten egg and bring it up over the tuna to enclose the fish completely, trimming off any bulky areas.

❺ Place the parcel, join side down, on a lightly greased baking sheet and brush with more egg. Bake in a preheated oven, 200°C (400°F), Gas Mark 6, for 30 minutes or until deep golden.

Fish pie

A good fish pie is a classic, comforting dish that never goes out of fashion. Keep it simple, using just the cod, or dress it up with more luxurious ingredients, such as scallops or prawns.

Preparation time 30 minutes
Cooking time 1 hour
Serves 6

1 kg (2 lb) cod fillet, skinned
3 tablespoons milk
275 g (9 oz) scallops or raw peeled prawns
1.25 kg (2½ lb) floury potatoes, thinly sliced
25 g (1 oz) butter
3 large shallots, finely chopped
4 tablespoons chopped tarragon
4 tablespoons chopped parsley
125 g (4 oz) Gruyère cheese, grated
1 quantity Béchamel Sauce (see page 20)
salt and pepper

❶ Put the cod in a frying pan with the milk and seasoning. Cover and cook gently for 5 minutes. Add the scallops or prawns and cook, covered, for a further 2 minutes. Drain, reserving the liquid, and leave to cool.

❷ Bring a saucepan of lightly salted water to the boil. Add the potatoes to the pan, return to the boil and cook for 6–8 minutes or until just tender. Drain. Melt the butter in the rinsed-out frying pan and fry the shallots for 5 minutes. Stir in the herbs.

❸ Flake the fish into large chunks, discarding any bones, and arrange the pieces in a large, shallow, ovenproof dish. Add the scallops or prawns, shallots and herbs.

❹ Stir two-thirds of the cheese into the béchamel sauce along with the poaching juices. Pour half over the fish. Layer the potatoes over the top and pour over the remaining sauce.

❺ Scatter with the rest of the cheese and bake in a preheated oven, 190°C (375°F), Gas Mark 5, for about 40 minutes or until golden.

Brazilian baked snapper

This colourful dish envelops the fish in spicy, aromatic flavours. If red snapper is not available use red bream, red mullet or sea bream instead.

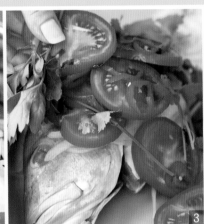

Preparation time 20 minutes, plus soaking and marinating

Cooking time 1¾ hours

Serves 4

250 g (8 oz) black beans

1 kg (2 lb) red snapper, scaled and gutted

juice of 1 lime

3 garlic cloves, chopped

3 bay leaves

2 onions, thinly sliced

4 tablespoons olive oil

several sprigs of parsley

25 g (1 oz) fresh coriander

200 g (7 oz) tomatoes, sliced

1 mild red chilli, deseeded and thinly sliced

salt and pepper

❶ Soak the beans overnight in cold water. Season the fish and drizzle it inside and out with the lime juice. Chill for 1 hour.

❷ Drain the beans, put them in a saucepan with plenty of water and bring to the boil. Boil rapidly for 10 minutes. Drain and return to the pan with the garlic, bay leaves, three-quarters of the sliced onions and 600 ml (1 pint) water. Bring to the boil, reduce the heat and simmer gently, uncovered, for 1½ hours or until tender.

❸ Meanwhile, lightly oil a shallow ovenproof dish and lay the fish in it. Cover the fish with the parsley and a few coriander sprigs, the tomatoes, chilli and remaining onion. Drizzle with the remaining oil and bake in a preheated oven, 200°C (400°F), Gas Mark 6, for 35 minutes or until cooked through.

❹ Drain the fish to a warm plate and tip the contents of the dish into a blender. Add the remaining coriander and blend until smooth. Reheat and season to taste. Serve with the beans and fish.

Salmon and crab fishcakes

Some fish recipes are best left quite simple, letting a few quality ingredients speak for themselves. Leave out the crab meat and add an extra potato for an everyday version.

Preparation time 25 minutes
Cooking time 30 minutes
Serves 4

700 g (1 lb 7 oz) baking potatoes
350 g (11½ oz) skinned salmon fillet
4 tablespoons milk
25 g (1 oz) butter
150 g (5 oz) dressed crab meat
2 tablespoons chopped tarragon
2 tablespoons chopped parsley
2 tablespoons capers, rinsed and drained
1 egg, beaten
flour, for dusting
mild olive oil, for shallow-frying
salt and pepper
crème fraîche, to serve

1 Cook the potatoes in plenty of lightly salted boiling water until tender. Meanwhile, put the salmon in a frying pan, pour over the milk, cover and cook gently for 8–10 minutes or until cooked through.

2 Drain the potatoes and return to the pan. Use a potato masher to crush the potatoes, leaving them in slightly chunky pieces. Stir in the butter.

3 When it is cool enough to handle, flake the salmon into chunky pieces, reserving the pan juices and checking for any bones. Add the fish and pan juices to the potatoes with the crab meat, herbs, capers, beaten egg and a little seasoning. Beat well until combined.

4 Shape the mixture into 8 equal balls, packing the mixture firmly together, then flatten them into cakes.

5 Heat a little oil in a heavy-based frying pan and fry the cakes, in 2 batches, for about 3 minutes on each side until golden. Serve hot with crème fraîche.

Smoked haddock crêpes

Succulent pieces of fish, bathed in a creamy cheese sauce and rolled up in pancakes, make a comforting supper dish. If you prefer, use firm-fleshed, unsmoked white fish instead.

Preparation time 40 minutes
Cooking time 50 minutes
Serves 4

125 g (4 oz) plain flour
1 egg
300 ml (½ pint) milk, plus 4 tablespoons
450 g (14½ oz) undyed smoked haddock
groundnut oil, for shallow-frying
200 g (7 oz) baby spinach
1 quantity Rich Cheese Sauce (add 50 g/2 oz grated Cheddar cheese to Béchamel Sauce, see page 20)
25 g (1 oz) Parmesan cheese, grated
salt and pepper

1 Make the batter. Whisk together the flour, egg and 150 ml (¼ pint) milk in a bowl until smooth. Whisk in another 150 ml (¼ pint) milk.

2 Cook the haddock in 4 tablespoons milk in a frying pan, covered, for 8–10 minutes. Leave to cool.

3 Heat a little oil in a crêpe pan until it begins to smoke. Wipe off the excess with kitchen paper and pour a little batter into the pan, tilting it to coat the base. Cook until the edges curl and the crêpe is cooked on the underside. Flip over and cook the other side briefly. Slide on to a plate and cook the remainder.

4 Wilt the spinach in a covered saucepan with 1 tablespoon water. Drain. Flake the fish, discarding the skin and any bones. Reserve one-third of the cheese sauce and stir the fish into the remainder. Scatter each crêpe with spinach, spoon a little of the fish and sauce down the centre and season lightly.

5 Roll up and arrange in a line in a shallow, ovenproof dish. Spoon over the remaining sauce and sprinkle with the grated Parmesan. Bake in a preheated oven, 190°C (375°F), Gas Mark 5, for 20–25 minutes.

Rouille

This fiery Mediterranean sauce is traditionally served with fish soups and bouillabaisse. A quick-and-easy version can be made by beating crushed garlic and chilli into ready-made mayonnaise.

Preparation time 15 minutes, plus chilling
Cooking time 15 minutes
Serves 6

1 large red pepper, deseeded
3 garlic cloves, roughly chopped
1 hot red chilli, deseeded and roughly chopped
1 egg yolk
25 g (1 oz) breadcrumbs
150 ml (¼ pint) olive oil
salt

❶ Cut the pepper into thick strips. Heat a griddle until very hot, then add the pepper strips, skin side down, and cook for about 15 minutes, turning frequently until the skin is blackened and charred. Alternatively, cook under a conventional grill. Leave to cool slightly, then peel away the skin.

❷ Put the pepper into a food processor or blender with the garlic, chilli, egg yolk and a little salt and blend to a paste, scraping down the mixture from the sides of the bowl if necessary.

❸ Add the breadcrumbs and 2 tablespoons oil and blend again to a paste.

❹ Gradually pour in the remaining oil in a thin trickle to make a sauce with a smooth consistency. Add a little more salt, if liked, then turn the sauce into a small serving dish. Cover and chill for up to 2 days before using.

Thermidor sauce

Traditionally served with lobster, this creamy sauce is also good with almost any shellfish or white fish but, like all stock-based sauces, it's only worth making with really good-quality fish stock.

Preparation time 15 minutes
Cooking time 25 minutes
Serves 6

400 ml (14 fl oz) Fish Stock (see page 19)
200 ml (7 fl oz) dry white wine
1 bouquet garni
15 g (½ oz) butter
15 g (½ oz) plain flour
300 ml (½ pint) full-cream milk
2 teaspoons tomato paste
1 teaspoon English mustard
¼ teaspoon cayenne pepper
1 tablespoon finely chopped chervil or tarragon
150 ml (¼ pint) double cream
1 tablespoon brandy
salt

1 Put the fish stock, wine and bouquet garni into a large, heavy-based saucepan and bring to the boil. Cook until the stock has reduced to 200 ml (7 fl oz).

2 In a separate heavy-based saucepan melt the butter until bubbling. Add the flour and cook, whisking, for 2 minutes until it is just beginning to colour. Remove from the heat and gradually blend in the milk, stirring until smooth. Return to the heat, add the tomato paste, mustard and cayenne pepper and bring to the boil. Simmer, stirring, for 5 minutes or until thickened.

3 Remove the bouquet garni from the stock and pour the stock into the sauce.

4 Stir in the chervil or tarragon, cream and brandy and let the sauce bubble until it thinly coats the back of a wooden spoon. Check the seasoning and serve hot.

Sauce vièrge

This is an incredibly pretty, fresh-looking sauce that's easy to make but looks impressive for summer entertaining. The herbs balance strong flavours, such as roasted monkfish or clams.

Preparation time 10 minutes

Cooking time 2 minutes

Serves 6

4 ripe tomatoes, skinned (see page 17)

½ teaspoon coriander seeds

15 g (½ oz) fresh herbs, such as chervil, flat leaf parsley, tarragon and chives

1 garlic clove, finely chopped

finely grated rind and juice of 1 lemon

100 ml (3½ fl oz) olive oil

salt and pepper

❶ Halve the tomatoes and scoop out the seeds with a teaspoon. Chop the flesh into small dice.

❷ Use a pestle and mortar to crush the coriander seeds as finely as possible. Discard the stalks from the herbs and finely chop the leaves. In a bowl mix together the diced tomatoes, coriander seeds, herbs, garlic, lemon rind and juice.

❸ Pour in the oil and season with a little salt and pepper. Cover and chill until ready to serve.

❹ Tip the sauce into a small saucepan and heat through gently until hot.

Tarragon cream sauce

This sauce uses the same method as béchamel sauce, but stock is used instead of milk. The result, a velouté sauce, can be flavoured with fresh herbs and is perfect with steamed mussels.

Preparation time 10 minutes
Cooking time 15 minutes
Serves 6

25 g (1 oz) butter
25 g (1 oz) plain flour
500 ml (17 fl oz) Fish Stock (see page 19)
8 large sprigs of tarragon
150 ml (¼ pint) dry white wine
½ teaspoon medium curry paste
4 tablespoons crème fraîche or single cream
salt and pepper

1 Melt the butter in a heavy-based saucepan until bubbling. Tip in the flour and cook gently, stirring with a wooden spoon, for 3–4 minutes or until the roux is golden-brown.

2 Remove the pan from the heat and gradually blend in the fish stock, stirring until smooth. Return the pan to the heat and bring to the boil, stirring. Reduce the heat and simmer gently, stirring until the sauce thinly coats the back of a wooden spoon.

3 Pull the tarragon leaves from the stalks and roughly chop the leaves.

4 Add the tarragon to the sauce with the wine, curry paste, crème fraîche or cream and a little salt and pepper and let the sauce bubble for about 5 minutes until it is smooth and glossy. Serve hot.

Parsley sauce

Traditional parsley sauce, made with really fresh, fragrant parsley, is an old-fashioned favourite that adapts well to any simply steamed or poached fish, such as salmon, hake or cod.

Preparation time 10 minutes

Cooking time 10 minutes

Serves 4

15 g (½ oz) curly parsley

250 ml (8 fl oz) Fish Stock (see page 19)

25 g (1 oz) butter

25 g (1 oz) plain flour

250 ml (8 fl oz) milk

3 tablespoons single cream

salt and pepper

1 Discard any tough stalks from the parsley and put it into a food processor or blender with half the stock. Blend until the parsley is very finely chopped.

2 Melt the butter in a heavy-based saucepan until bubbling. Tip in the flour and stir quickly to combine. Cook the mixture gently, stirring constantly with a wooden spoon, for 2 minutes.

3 Remove the pan from the heat and gradually whisk in the parsley-flavoured stock, then the remaining stock, until smooth. Whisk in the milk. Return to the heat and bring to the boil, stirring. Reduce the heat and continue to cook the sauce for about 5 minutes, stirring frequently, until it is smooth and glossy. The sauce should thinly coat the back of the spoon.

4 Stir in the cream and a little salt and pepper and heat gently to warm through. Serve with steamed or poached fish.

MEAT, POULTRY AND GAME

Steak meatloaf

Serve this meatloaf hot or cold, depending on the weather and circumstances. Leftovers, accompanied with salad and chutney, make an ideal lunchtime snack.

Preparation time 30 minutes
Cooking time 2½ hours
Serves 6

2 red peppers, deseeded and cut into chunks
1 red onion, sliced
3 tablespoons olive oil
300 g (10 oz) thin-cut streaky bacon
500 g (1 lb) lean steak mince
250 g (8 oz) pork mince
2 tablespoons chopped oregano
2 tablespoons chopped flat leaf parsley
3 tablespoons Worcestershire sauce
2 tablespoons sun-dried tomato paste
50 g (2 oz) breadcrumbs
1 egg
salt and pepper

1 Scatter the peppers and onion in a roasting tin and drizzle with the oil. Cook in a preheated oven, 200°C (400°F), Gas Mark 6, for 30 minutes until lightly roasted, then chop. Reduce the oven temperature to 160°C (325°F), Gas Mark 3.

2 Meanwhile, line the base and long sides of a 1 kg (2 lb) loaf tin with some bacon, overlapping the pieces and letting the ends overhang the sides. Chop the rest.

3 Mix together both minces, the chopped bacon, roasted vegetables, herbs, Worcestershire sauce, tomato paste, breadcrumbs, egg and seasoning.

4 Pack the mixture into the tin and fold the ends of the bacon over the filling. Cover with foil, place in a roasting tin and pour in 2 cm (¾ inch) boiling water. Cook in the oven for 2 hours. To serve hot leave for 15 minutes, then invert on to a serving plate. To serve cold leave to cool in the tin, remove and wrap in foil.

Steak and chips with béarnaise sauce

If you're going to indulge in a prime steak, it's worth making a bit of an effort over these 'shoestring' chips.

Preparation time 20 minutes

Cooking time 20–30 minutes

Serves 4

500 g (1 lb) floury potatoes, such as Maris Piper

15 g (½ oz) chopped tarragon or chervil

2 shallots, finely chopped

3 tablespoons white wine vinegar

1 teaspoon black peppercorns

3 egg yolks

200 g (7 oz) unsalted butter, cut into cubes, plus 15 g (½ oz)
vegetable oil, for frying

4 steaks, such as sirloin, fillet, rump or T-bone

salt and pepper

❶ Slice the potatoes 5 mm (¼ inch) thick, then across into matchstick-sized chips. Put in a bowl of cold water. Put a quarter of the herbs in a small saucepan with the shallots, vinegar, peppercorns and 1 tablespoon water. Cook until reduced to 1 tablespoon.

❷ Heat a little water in a medium-sized pan until simmering. Put the egg yolks in a heatproof bowl over the pan, making sure the base of the bowl does not touch the water. Strain the vinegar mixture into the bowl. Add a cube of butter and whisk into the sauce until melted. Keep adding the butter, a cube at a time, until the sauce is thick and glossy. Stir in the remaining chopped herbs and season to taste. Turn off the heat, cover and leave to stand.

❸ Drain the chips and pat dry on kitchen paper. Pour 8 cm (3 inches) of oil into a deep fryer or large, heavy-based saucepan and heat until a chip sizzles on the surface. Add half the chips and fry for about 5 minutes until soft but not golden. Drain and fry the remainder.

❹ Melt the butter in a frying pan or griddle. Season the steaks and fry, turning once, until cooked to your liking (see page 35). Return all the chips to the hot oil and fry for 2–3 minutes until deep golden. Drain well and serve.

Fillet of beef with walnuts

Requiring little preparation, this steak recipe is pretty much unbeatable. It can be made ahead, including the gravy, ready for a quick blast in a hot oven before serving.

Preparation time 20 minutes
Cooking time 20 minutes
Serves 6

50 g (2 oz) butter
3 shallots, finely chopped
3 garlic cloves, crushed
2 teaspoons chopped rosemary
125 g (4 oz) walnut pieces, roughly chopped
125 g (4 oz) pickled walnuts, drained and roughly chopped
1 tablespoon hot horseradish sauce
1 kg (2 lb) piece fillet of beef
1 tablespoon olive oil
300 ml (½ pint) Beef or Chicken Stock (see page 18)
1 large glass red wine
salt and pepper
chopped flat leaf parsley, to garnish

❶ Melt half the butter in a large, heavy-based frying pan and fry the shallots for 3–4 minutes or until softened. Stir in the garlic and rosemary, tip the mixture into a bowl and add all the walnuts, the horseradish sauce and a little seasoning.

❷ Cut the beef into 6 equal pieces and season. Melt the remaining butter with the oil in the frying pan and sear the steaks on all sides. Transfer to a roasting tin, leaving the frying pan to one side.

❸ Pile the walnut mixture on the steaks and press down gently. Cook in a preheated oven, 200°C (400°F), Gas Mark 6, for 10 minutes.

❹ Meanwhile, pour the stock and wine into the frying pan and bring to the boil, stirring to scrape up any residue. Let the mixture bubble until reduced by about half. Transfer the steaks to warm plates, pour over a little sauce and scatter with parsley.

Beefburgers with chilli and avocado salsa

Nothing beats homemade burgers, served with a fresh, tangy salsa, either in buns or with chunky chips. This recipe makes four large burgers, but shape them into eight smaller, flatter ones if you like.

Preparation time 15 minutes
Cooking time 10–12 minutes
Serves 6

750 g (1½ lb) lean minced steak
½ small onion, finely chopped
25 g (1 oz) breadcrumbs
1 egg, beaten
vegetable oil, for frying
salt and pepper

Salsa
2 tablespoons sweet chilli sauce
1 tablespoon lime juice
½ small red onion, finely chopped
1 avocado

1 Put the mince, onion, breadcrumbs, egg and a little seasoning in a bowl and mix together until thoroughly combined. This is most easily done with your hands but use a wooden spoon if you prefer.

2 Divide the mixture into 6 and roll each portion into a ball. Flatten them into burger shapes, about 2.5 cm (1 inch) thick.

3 Make the salsa by mixing together the chilli sauce, lime juice and onion in a bowl. Halve, stone and peel the avocado. Finely chop the flesh and mix it with the chilli sauce mixture.

4 Brush a large, heavy-based frying pan with oil and gently fry the burgers for 5–6 minutes on each side or until cooked through. Serve topped with the salsa.

Roast beef and Yorkshire puddings

If you are cooking roast potatoes, use a separate tin and put it on the top shelf of the oven for the final hour's roasting. Move them to the lower shelf while the Yorkshire puddings cook.

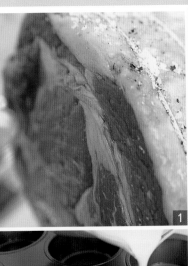

Preparation time 20 minutes
Cooking time 1¼–2½ hours
Serves 6–8

1.5–2 kg (3–4 lb) rib or sirloin of beef, on the bone or boned and rolled
dripping or lard
150 ml (¼ pint) Beef Stock (see page 18)
150 ml (¼ pint) red wine
salt and pepper

Yorkshire puddings
125 g (4 oz) plain flour
2 eggs
300 ml (½ pint) milk

❶ Weigh the meat and calculate the cooking time (see page 34). Put it in a roasting tin with the fat uppermost and rub all over with a little seasoning. Roast in a preheated oven, 220°C (425°F), Gas Mark 7, for 15 minutes. Reduce the oven temperature to 180°C (350°F), Gas Mark 4, and cook for the calculated time.

❷ Meanwhile, make the pudding batter. Mix the flour with a little salt in a bowl and break the eggs into the centre. Add half the milk and gradually whisk in the flour and then the remaining milk to make a smooth batter. Leave to stand.

❸ Transfer the beef to a serving platter, cover and leave to stand. Increase the oven temperature to 220°C (425°F), Gas Mark 7. Dot a little lard or dripping (or fat from the roasting tin) into sections of a Yorkshire pudding tin and put it in the oven until very hot. Pour in the batter and cook for 20–25 minutes until risen and golden.

❹ Heat the stock and wine in the tin with the meat juices, scraping up the residue. Bring to the boil and pour into a jug.

Mexican chilli

Although it's not authentically Mexican, chilli con carne is a deliciously spicy bean stew, which benefits from slow and gentle cooking. This version uses diced braising steak.

Preparation time 20 minutes, plus soaking
Cooking time 1 hour 40 minutes
Serves 6

250 g (8 oz) dried red or black kidney beans
750 g (1½ lb) lean braising steak, diced
3 tablespoons olive oil
2 onions, chopped
1 tablespoon mild chilli powder
1 tablespoon cumin seeds, crushed
1 teaspoon celery salt
3 garlic cloves, crushed
2 tablespoons dark muscovado sugar
1 glass red wine
150 ml (¼ pint) Beef or Chicken Stock (see page 18)
2 x 400 g (13 oz) cans chopped tomatoes
salt and pepper
crème fraîche, to serve
chopped coriander, to garnish

1 Cover the beans with cold water and leave them to soak overnight. Drain and put them in a large saucepan with fresh water. Bring to the boil and boil rapidly for 10 minutes. Drain and reserve.

2 Season the steak. Heat the oil in a large, heavy-based saucepan and fry the beef in 2 batches until well browned. Drain and remove from the pan.

3 Add the onions to the pan with the chilli powder, cumin seeds and celery salt and fry gently for 5 minutes. Add the garlic and sugar and fry for 1 minute.

4 Return the beef to the pan with the wine, stock, tomatoes and beans. Heat until bubbling, then reduce the heat and simmer, covered, for 1¼ hours until the meat is tender. Serve with crème fraîche and coriander.

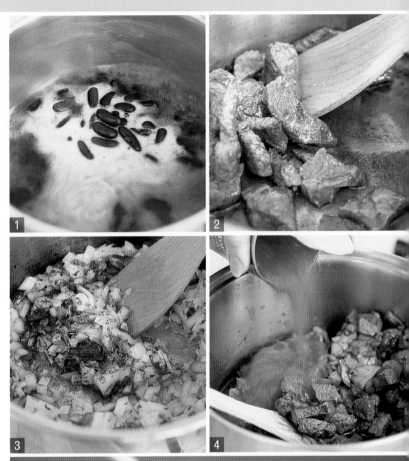

Veal saltimbocca

Bashed thin, veal escalopes are quick to cook and stay moist and tender. This recipe is easy enough for the 'not-so-keen cook' and produces delicious results every time.

Preparation time 10 minutes
Cooking time 10 minutes
Serves 4

8 small veal escalopes
2 teaspoons plain flour
50 g (2 oz) butter
8 slices of prosciutto
8 large sage leaves
250 ml (8 fl oz) dry white wine
salt and pepper

❶ Place the veal escalopes between 2 layers of clingfilm and beat them with a rolling pin or meat mallet until they are very thin. Season the flour and use it to dust the meat.

❷ Melt 25 g (1 oz) butter in a large, heavy-based frying pan and quickly fry the veal, in batches, until lightly browned, draining the meat and transferring the slices to a plate.

❸ Lay a slice of prosciutto and 1 sage leaf on the centre of each escalope and return them to the pan for a further 2–3 minutes until cooked through, carefully turning each escalope once to sear the prosciutto and sage. Drain and transfer to warm serving plates.

❹ Pour the wine into the pan and let it bubble until reduced by about half. Cut the remaining butter into pieces and whisk into the wine. Season to taste and pour the sauce over the escalopes to serve.

Spicy maple ribs

Lengthy cooking ensures that the pork falls easily from the bone and the juices bake to a deliciously dark, sticky glaze. Serve the ribs with a watercress or other dark leaf salad and chunky chips.

Preparation time 10 minutes, plus marinating
Cooking time 1½–1¾ hours
Serves 4

1.25 kg (2½ lb) meaty pork spare ribs
100 ml (3½ fl oz) maple syrup
2 garlic cloves, crushed
3 tablespoons white wine vinegar
3 tablespoons tomato paste
finely grated rind and juice of 1 lemon
1 red chilli, deseeded and finely chopped
½ teaspoon smoked paprika
salt
lemon or lime halves, to serve

❶ Arrange the meat in a single layer in a shallow, non-metallic dish. Beat together the maple syrup, garlic, wine vinegar, tomato paste, lemon rind and juice, chilli and paprika.

❷ Pour the mixture over the ribs, turning them until they are completely coated. Cover and marinate in the refrigerator for 4–24 hours.

❸ Transfer the ribs to a shallow roasting tin and pour over the excess marinade from the dish.

❹ Season lightly with salt and bake in a preheated oven, 180°C (350°F), Gas Mark 4, for 1½–1¾ hours, basting occasionally with the juices, until the meat is tender and the juices are thick and sticky. Transfer to serving plates and serve with lemon or lime halves for squeezing over.

Mustard sausages with sweet potato mash

Use good-quality, lean pork sausages for this recipe. Those with added herbs and garlic are ideal, balancing the sweetness of the mango chutney glaze.

Preparation time 20 minutes
Cooking time 45 minutes
Serves 4

4 tablespoons mango chutney
4 teaspoons grainy mustard
finely grated rind and juice of ½ lemon
500 g (1 lb) lean pork sausages
2 red onions, thinly sliced
2 tablespoons vegetable oil
750 g (1½ lb) sweet potatoes
500 g (1 lb) swede
25 g (1 oz) butter
100 ml (3½ fl oz) Chicken Stock (see page 18) or water
pepper

1 Finely chop any pieces in the chutney and mix together the chutney, mustard and lemon rind and juice in a small bowl. Put the sausages in a roasting tin and brush them with the mixture.

2 Scatter the onions into the tin and drizzle with the oil. Cook in a preheated oven, 180°C (350°F), Gas Mark 4, for about 45 minutes, basting the sausages once or twice with the juices, until golden.

3 Meanwhile, scrub the sweet potatoes and cut them into chunks. Cut away the skin from the swede and cut the flesh into chunks. Cook the vegetables in separate pans until tender. Drain thoroughly, transfer to one pan and add the butter and a little black pepper. Mash well.

4 Pile the mash, sausages and onions on to warm serving plates. Pour the stock into the roasting tin and heat until bubbling, scraping up the residue from the tin. Pour over the mash and serve.

Italian sausage and onion tart

Keep the paper-thin sheets of filo pastry covered with clingfilm or a damp tea towel until you are ready to use them, to prevent them from drying out.

Preparation time 20 minutes
Cooking time 1 hour
Serves 4

3 tablespoons olive oil
6 Italian sausages
2 red onions, cut into wedges
6 sheets filo pastry
100 g (3½ oz) mascarpone cheese
50 g (2 oz) Roquefort cheese
3 large eggs
2 tablespoons milk
1 tablespoon wholegrain mustard
chives, to garnish

❶ Heat 1 tablespoon oil in a frying pan and cook the sausages and onions over a medium heat for about 15 minutes or until they are browned and cooked. Leave to one side.

❷ Brush the filo sheets with the remaining oil. Line a 35 x 12 cm (14 x 5 inch) loose-based tart tin with the pastry, overlapping the sheets and allowing them to overhang the sides. Bunch up the overhanging pastry to make a rim around the edges. Bake in a preheated oven, 180°C (350°F), Gas Mark 4, for 10 minutes or until the base is dry. Leave the oven on.

❸ Whisk together the mascarpone, Roquefort, eggs, milk and mustard to make a smooth mixture. Pour it into the base of the tart.

❹ Arrange the sausages and onion wedges evenly over the batter. Bake for 30–35 minutes or until golden and set. Serve warm, garnished with fresh chives.

Asian roasted belly pork

A lean piece of belly pork will make a delicious yet inexpensive roasting joint. Serve it on a bed of rice with stir-fried vegetables.

Preparation time 15 minutes, plus standing

Cooking time 1 hour 10 minutes

Serves 5–6

1.5 kg (3 lb) piece belly pork, boned and skinned

1 teaspoon sea salt

½ teaspoon crushed dried chillies

1 teaspoon coriander seeds

2 whole star anise, broken into pieces

½ cinnamon stick, crumbled

8 whole cloves

2 teaspoons caster sugar

2 tablespoons sesame oil

4 small onions, thinly sliced

4 garlic cloves, crushed

4 tablespoons clear honey

3 tablespoons hoisin sauce

1 Use a large, sharp knife to score the pork fat at 1 cm (½ inch) intervals, then score it across in the opposite direction.

2 Grind the salt and spices with the sugar in a food processor or coffee grinder. Brush a roasting tin with 1 teaspoon oil and put the meat in, scored side up. Rub the spice blend thoroughly into the fat. Cook in a preheated oven, 200°C (400°F), Gas Mark 6, for 30 minutes. Leave the oven on.

3 Mix the onions with the garlic and remaining oil and spoon them around the pork. Brush the pork with 2 tablespoons honey. Roast for a further 20 minutes. Brush with the remaining honey and cook for a further 20 minutes until the pork is deep golden.

4 Drain the pork and transfer it to a board. Add the hoisin sauce and 100 ml (3½ fl oz) water to the roasting tin and bring to the boil, stirring. Carve the meat and serve with the sauce.

Pan-fried pork with squash

Any pork steaks work well in this dish, so choose the best available when you buy. Use any type of squash; butternut works particularly well.

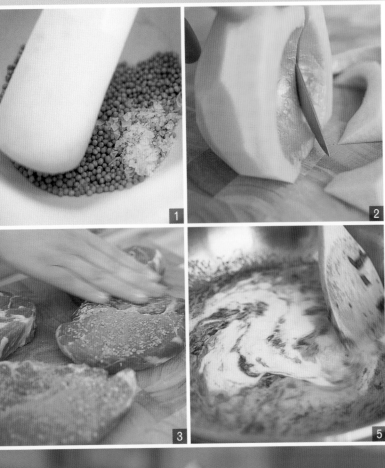

Preparation time 15 minutes
Cooking time about 30 minutes
Serves 4

2 teaspoons mustard seeds
¼ teaspoon sea salt
500 g (1 lb) squash
4 boneless pork steaks, such as leg, chump or shoulder
25 g (1 oz) butter
1 tablespoon vegetable oil
1 tablespoon chopped sage
150 ml (¼ pint) Chicken Stock (see page 18)
100 ml (3½ fl oz) crème fraîche

❶ Put the mustard seeds in a small, heavy-based frying pan and heat gently until they start to pop or toast. Use a pestle and mortar to crush them lightly with the salt.

❷ Cut away the skin from the squash and scoop out any seeds. Cut the squash into chunky slices.

❸ Pat the pork dry on kitchen paper and rub the mustard and salt over the top of the steaks.

❹ Melt the butter with the oil in a large, heavy-based frying pan and fry the squash on both sides until golden and tender. Drain, transfer to a plate and keep warm. Add the steaks, spiced side down, and fry for 6–8 minutes or until golden. Turn the steaks and add the sage and stock. Cook gently for a further 6–8 minutes or until cooked through. Drain and keep warm.

❺ Stir the crème fraîche into the pan and cook, stirring, until it is bubbling and slightly thickened. Check the seasoning and serve with the pork and squash.

Glazed ham

A large joint of gammon does well for family eating (hot one day, cold the next) or for a festive dinner. If you are serving the ham hot, cook potatoes and carrots in the poaching liquid.

Preparation time 15 minutes, plus soaking
Cooking time 2 hours 20 minutes–3 hours
Serves 8–12

2.5 kg (5 lb) piece of gammon
2 onions, sliced
2 carrots, roughly chopped
2 celery sticks, roughly chopped
several sprigs of thyme
4 bay leaves
1 tablespoon peppercorns
8 whole star anise
2 tablespoons orange marmalade
75 g (3 oz) light muscovado sugar
6 kumquats, thinly sliced

1 Soak the gammon overnight in cold water. Drain and weigh to calculate cooking time, allowing 20 minutes per 500 g (1 lb).

2 Put the gammon in a saucepan into which it fits snugly and add the onions, carrots, celery, thyme, bay leaves, peppercorns and 3 of the star anise. Cover with cold water, bring to a simmer, then cover and cook gently for the calculated time. Leave to cool in the cooking liquid for 30 minutes.

3 Drain the meat to a board. Carefully cut away the rind, leaving a layer of fat. Cut diagonal lines across the fat, about 3 cm (1¼ inches) apart, then score lines in the opposite direction.

4 Melt the marmalade in a small pan and stir in the sugar. Spread the mixture over the scored meat. Arrange the kumquats and remaining star anise over the surface and put it in a foil-lined tin. Cook in a preheated oven, 200°C (400°F), Gas Mark 6, for about 20 minutes or until the sugar starts to caramelize. Leave to stand for 20 minutes before serving.

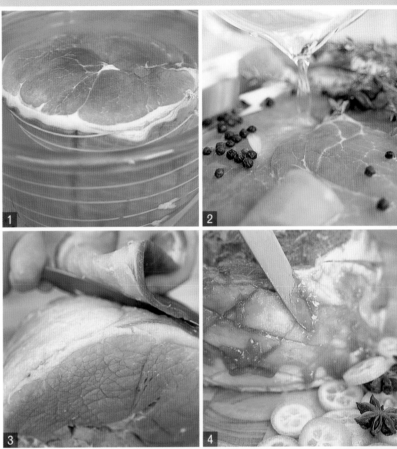

Filo tarts with red pepper and pancetta

If you cannot find spicy Italian pancetta use the best quality streaky bacon. Remember to keep the filo pastry covered with a damp tea towel or clingfilm so that it does not dry out.

Preparation time 10 minutes
Cooking time 36–38 minutes
Serves 6

18 squares, 11 x 11 cm (4½ x 4½ inches), cut from 6–8 sheets filo pastry

25 g (1 oz) butter, melted

1 tablespoon olive oil

125 g (4 oz) pancetta, diced

1 large red pepper, cored deseeded and roughly chopped

1 red onion, roughly chopped

1 teaspoon hot paprika

100 ml (3½ fl oz) passata

6 eggs

50 g (2 oz) Gruyère cheese, grated

❶ Brush the filo squares with melted butter and stick them together at different angles in piles of 3 so that you end up with 6 stacks. Push each stack into a 10 cm (4 inch) tart case and bake in a preheated oven, 200°C (400°F), Gas Mark 6, for 8–10 minutes. Leave the oven on.

❷ Heat the oil in a frying pan and fry the pancetta, red pepper, onion and paprika for 8 minutes until just cooked through.

❸ Remove from the heat and stir in the passata. Divide the mixture among the tart cases, making a well in the centre of each tart.

❹ Crack an egg into each well, sprinkle with the cheese and bake in the oven for 20 minutes.

Lamb with salmoriglio sauce

With their lemony, herb sauce these lamb chops are made for al fresco dining. Make the salmoriglio sauce several hours in advance so that the flavours have a chance to mingle.

Preparation time 10 minutes
Cooking time 15 minutes
Serves 4

8 loin of lamb chops or 4 large chump chops
1 tablespoon chopped fresh oregano
2 tablespoons chopped flat leaf parsley
1 tablespoon capers, drained, rinsed and chopped
1 teaspoon dried oregano
3 garlic cloves, crushed
finely grated rind and juice of 1 small lemon
150 ml (¼ pint) extra virgin olive oil, plus extra for cooking
salt and pepper

1 Trim any excess fat from the chops. If you are using loin chops tie each chop into a neat shape with string.

2 Mix the chopped oregano with the parsley and capers on a board.

3 Put the chopped herbs and capers in a bowl with the dried oregano, garlic, lemon rind and juice, oil and seasoning. Whisk well until combined.

4 Cook the chops under a preheated hot grill or in a lightly oiled griddle pan for 6–7 minutes on each side, brushing halfway through cooking with a little of the sauce. Serve with the remaining sauce.

Mediterranean roast lamb

Using a boned joint lets the flavours infuse the meat. This recipe gives a slightly pink result – for well done, cook the lamb at the lower temperature for 30 minutes before adding the potatoes.

Preparation time 25 minutes

Cooking time 2¼ hours

Serves 6

50 g (2 oz) sun-dried tomatoes in oil, drained

100 g (3½ oz) grilled aubergines in oil, drained

7 tablespoons olive oil

2 red onions, chopped separately

6 garlic cloves, thinly sliced

75 g (3 oz) pine nuts

1 leg of lamb, about 1.5 kg (3 lb), part boned

1.5 kg (3 lb) large potatoes, cut into 2 cm (¾ inch) chunks

1 tablespoon chopped rosemary

300 ml (½ pint) Lamb Stock (see page 18) or white wine

salt and pepper

❶ Finely chop the tomatoes and aubergines. Heat 2 tablespoons oil in a frying pan and fry 1 onion until soft. Add the tomatoes, aubergines, half the garlic, half the pine nuts and the seasoning. Stir to mix.

❷ Stuff the lamb with tomato and aubergine mixture, using skewers to close. Blanch the potatoes in lightly salted boiling water for 5 minutes. Mix the remaining chopped onion and pine nuts and the rosemary with the rest of the oil. Toss with the potatoes and season to taste.

❸ Make small incisions over the lamb and insert a garlic slice into each. Roast the meat in a preheated oven, 220°C (425°F), Gas Mark 7, for 30 minutes. Surround with the potato mixture, reduce the heat to 160°C (325°F), Gas Mark 3, and cook for 1¼ hours, turning the potatoes once.

❹ Drain and transfer to a serving platter. Add the stock or wine to the pan. Boil, scraping up the residue, check the seasoning and serve.

Indian lamb with almond sauce

This recipe is like a quick and easy roghan josh with chunks of tender lamb in a richly spiced, nutty sauce. Like many spiced meat dishes, this reheats well.

Preparation time 25 minutes
Cooking time 1¼ hours
Serves 5–6

750 g (1½ lb) lamb neck fillet
10 whole cardamom pods
1 tablespoon cumin seeds
3 tablespoons vegetable oil
1 hot red chilli, deseeded and chopped
1 tablespoon desiccated coconut
50 g (2 oz) blanched almonds, chopped
40 g (1½ oz) fresh root ginger, peeled and grated
4 garlic cloves, chopped
1 teaspoon ground turmeric
1 onion, finely chopped
4 tablespoons natural yogurt
500 g (1 lb) tomatoes, skinned (see page 17) and chopped
salt
rice, to serve

❶ Cut the lamb into chunks, discarding any fat, and pat dry. Crush the cardamom and cumin seeds, discarding the cardamom shells. Heat the oil in a large, heavy-based frying pan and gently fry the chilli, cardamom and cumin.

❷ Add half the lamb and fry, stirring, until well browned. Drain and transfer the meat to a large saucepan. Fry the remaining lamb and add it to the pan.

❸ Add the coconut and almonds to the frying pan and fry until lightly browned. Tip into a blender or food processor with the ginger, garlic, turmeric, onion and 6 tablespoons water and blend to a paste. Return to the frying pan, add the yogurt and cook, stirring, for 5 minutes.

❹ Stir in another 150 ml (¼ pint) water and pour the mixture over the lamb. Add the tomatoes. Cover and cook on the lowest heat for about 1 hour or until the lamb is tender. Season to taste and serve with rice.

Rack of lamb with pineapple salsa

The tangy pineapple salsa gives this dish a fresh, summery flavour that's lovely served with steamed couscous. Use a very ripe pineapple, which is more likely to be sweet and tender.

Preparation time 10 minutes
Cooking time 25 minutes
Serves 4

2 teaspoons chopped thyme
2 French-trimmed racks of lamb, each about 550 g (1 lb 2 oz)
salt and pepper

Salsa
½ small pineapple
finely grated rind and juice of 1 lime
2 teaspoons golden caster sugar
1 spring onion, finely chopped
1 large, mild chilli, deseeded and sliced
3 tablespoons roughly chopped coriander

1 Mix the thyme with plenty of salt and pepper and rub it over the surface of the lamb. Fit the two racks together so that the bones interlock and place them in a roasting tin. Roast in a preheated oven, 200°C (400°F), Gas Mark 6, for 25 minutes. Cover and leave to stand for 15 minutes.

2 Meanwhile, make the salsa. Cut away the skin and core from the pineapple and finely chop the flesh.

3 Mix the lime rind and juice in a bowl with the sugar until the sugar dissolves. Tip in the pineapple, spring onion, chilli, coriander and a little salt and mix together. Turn into a small serving dish.

4 Transfer the lamb to a carving board and separate the racks. Cut the racks into single or double cutlets between the ribs. Arrange on warm serving plates and serve with the salsa.

Braised lamb shanks with vegetables

Allow at least a day, or preferably two, to marinate the meat so that it has plenty of time to become tenderized and to absorb all the marinade flavours.

Preparation time 25 minutes, plus marinating

Cooking time 2 hours

Serves 6

6 lamb shanks

2 onions

8 sprigs of thyme

2 bay leaves

2 teaspoons cocoa powder

450 ml (¾ pint) red wine

3 garlic cloves

1 teaspoon black peppercorns

4 tablespoons olive oil

200 g (7 oz) baby carrots

150 g (5 oz) broad beans

6 pickled walnuts, halved

25 g (1 oz) plain chocolate, chopped

parsley, to garnish

salt

❶ Put the lamb shanks in a large, shallow container into which they fit quite snugly. Roughly chop 1 onion and put it in a blender or food processor with the herbs, cocoa powder, wine, garlic and peppercorns. Blend until slightly pulpy and pour the mixture over the lamb. Cover and leave to marinate for 24–48 hours, turning the meat several times.

❷ Drain the lamb, reserving the marinade, and pat the meat dry on kitchen paper. Heat the oil in a large frying pan and fry the lamb, turning frequently, for about 10 minutes or until deep golden. Transfer the meat to a shallow ovenproof dish or roasting tin.

❸ Finely chop the remaining onion and fry in the pan for 3 minutes. Strain the marinade into the pan and bring to the boil. Pour it over the lamb and cover the dish with a lid or foil. Cook in a preheated oven, 160°C (325°F), Gas Mark 3, for 1½ hours or until the lamb is tender. Scatter the carrots, beans and pickled walnuts around the lamb and return to the oven for a further 15 minutes or until the vegetables are tender.

❹ Drain the meat and vegetables and transfer to serving plates. Stir the chocolate into the pan juices until melted. Check the seasoning and pour the sauce into a jug. Serve the lamb drizzled with the sauce and garnished with parsley.

Pot-roasted chicken with lentils

This dish makes a change from a more traditionally roasted chicken. Serve with roast potatoes and green vegetables or with a herb or tomato salad for a lighter meal.

Preparation time 15 minutes
Cooking time 2 hours
Serves 4

1.5 kg (3 lb) chicken
25 g (1 oz) butter
2 tablespoons olive oil
1 onion, sliced
3 celery sticks, sliced
4–6 garlic cloves, crushed
250 ml (8 fl oz) dry white wine
3 bay leaves
several sprigs of thyme
150 g (5 oz) puy lentils
2 tablespoons capers, rinsed
4 tablespoons chopped parsley
100 g (3½ oz) crème fraîche
salt and pepper

❶ Season the chicken with salt and pepper. Melt the butter with the oil in a frying pan and fry the chicken on all sides to brown. Transfer to a large casserole dish or a deep-sided roasting tin with a lid.

❷ Fry the onion and celery in the pan juices for 6–8 minutes or until lightly browned. Stir in the garlic, wine and herbs and pour the mixture over the chicken. Cover and bake in a preheated oven, 160°C (325°F), Gas Mark 3, for 1 hour.

❸ Meanwhile, rinse the lentils and put them in a saucepan with plenty of water. Bring to the boil and boil for 10 minutes. Drain well. Tip the lentils around the chicken and return to the oven for a further 45 minutes.

❹ Transfer the cooked chicken to a warm dish and cover it with foil. Stir in the capers, parsley and crème fraîche. Mix together, stirring until heated through. Check the seasoning and serve with the chicken.

Thai chicken curry

Like many Thai curries, this is quick and easy to make and bursting with lively, aromatic ingredients. Serve in bowls with fragrant Thai rice.

Preparation time 25 minutes
Cooking time 40 minutes
Serves 4

1 kg (2 lb) boned and skinned chicken thighs
300 ml (½ pint) Chicken Stock (see page 18)
400 ml (14 fl oz) can coconut milk
3 tablespoons vegetable oil

Curry paste
5 cm (2 inches) fresh galangal or fresh root ginger
1 hot red chilli, deseeded and sliced
1 stalk lemon grass
2 garlic cloves, sliced
1 small onion, roughly chopped
small handful of fresh coriander
1 teaspoon shrimp paste
½ teaspoon ground turmeric
1 teaspoon cumin seeds
2 teaspoons dark brown sugar
pinch of salt

1 Make the curry paste. Peel and roughly chop the galangal or ginger and put it in a blender or food processor with the remaining paste ingredients. Blend to a paste, scraping the mixture down from the sides of the bowl when necessary.

2 Slice the chicken into small pieces and put them in a heavy-based saucepan with the stock and coconut milk. Bring slowly to the boil, then reduce the heat to its lowest setting and cook gently for 30 minutes.

3 Heat the oil in a frying pan and fry the curry paste until it is beginning to colour.

4 Stir 2 ladlefuls of the coconut milk mixture into the paste, blending it in until smooth, then pour the mixture over the chicken. Simmer gently for 5 minutes. Check the seasoning and serve.

Crispy aromatic duck

This is a simplified version of the traditional technique for cooking an aromatic, tender Chinese duck. It's gently oven-steamed to make it moist and succulent before a final roasting.

Preparation time 30 minutes, plus marinating

Cooking time 3½ hours

Serves 4

2.1 kg (4½ lb) Peking duck

1 tablespoon Sichuan peppercorns

2 tablespoons five-spice powder

2 tablespoons sea salt

4 tablespoons vegetable oil

8 Chinese pancakes

hoisin sauce

½ cucumber, cut into fine matchsticks

1 bunch of spring onions, finely shredded

① Rinse the duck and pat it dry with kitchen paper. Grind the peppercorns and mix with the five-spice powder and salt. Rub the mixture over the duck, wrap in clingfilm and leave it in the refrigerator overnight.

② Fit a rack over a roasting tin and put the duck on top. Pour hot water to a depth of 5 cm (2 inches) into the tin and cover the duck with a tent of foil. Carefully transfer to a preheated oven, 150°C (300°F), Gas Mark 2, and cook for 2½ hours. Increase the heat to 180°C (350°F), Gas Mark 4.

③ Pour away the liquid from the tin and reposition the duck. Brush with the oil and return to the oven, uncovered, for 1 hour or until the skin is crisp.

④ Leave to stand for 20 minutes then cut off the meat, shredding it into small pieces. Reheat the pancakes according to the instructions on the packet and serve with the duck, hoisin sauce and vegetables.

Duck confit

Confit, meaning preserve, is the traditional French way of keeping duck without refrigeration for several months. If you are short of goose fat make up the quantity with a little lard.

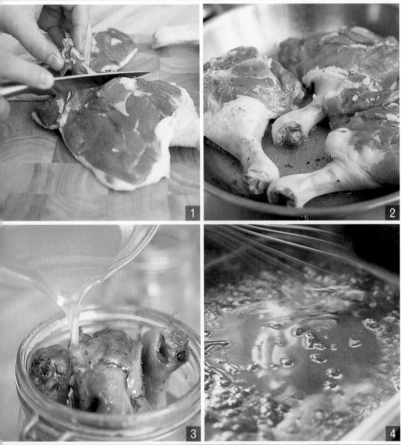

Preparation time 30 minutes, plus chilling
Cooking time 2 hours
Serves 6

6 large duck legs, each about 300 g (10 oz)
25 g (1 oz) sea salt
1 teaspoon finely chopped thyme
6 garlic cloves, crushed
625 g (1¼ lb) duck or goose fat
2 shallots, finely chopped
300 ml (½ pint) port
100 ml (3½ fl oz) freshly squeezed orange juice
black pepper

❶ Cut through the joint of each duck leg. Scrape away the thigh bone and discard. Mix together the salt, thyme and garlic, season with pepper and rub the mixture into the skin of each leg. Cover and chill for 24–48 hours.

❷ Scrape the salt off and reserve. Melt 1 tablespoon fat in a heavy-based pan and fry the legs on both sides until golden. Drain into a small casserole dish into which they fit snugly. Add the reserved salt mixture and fat. (If the fat is solid melt it gently before adding.) Cover and cook in a preheated oven, 150°C (300°F), Gas Mark 2, for 1½ hours. Leave to cool in the fat.

❸ Drain the legs to a container. Cover with the fat and chill or store in a very cool place for up to 2 months.

❹ Scoop the duck from the fat, scraping off as much as possible, and put in a roasting tin. Cook in a preheated oven, 200°C (400°F), Gas Mark 6, for 20 minutes or until heated through. Drain the fat from the tin and fry the shallots until softened. Add the port and orange juice and cook until reduced by two-thirds. Season and spoon over the duck.

Marinated duck with ginger sauce

Although distinctively chocolaty, this fabulous sauce has a fresh
tang that's the perfect complement for the richness of the duck.

Preparation time 20 minutes, plus marinating
Cooking time 40 minutes
Serves 4

4 large duck breasts

1 onion, sliced

1 celery stick, chopped

4 tablespoons clear honey

50 g (2 oz) fresh root ginger, peeled and grated

3 tablespoons lemon juice

1 tablespoon soy sauce

2 teaspoons five-spice powder

1 tablespoon groundnut oil

15 g (½ oz) plain chocolate, chopped

❶ Score each piece of duck several times with a sharp
knife. Scatter the onion and celery in a shallow, non-
metallic dish and place the duck on top.

❷ Mix together the honey, ginger, lemon juice, soy sauce
and five-spice powder and pour it over the duck. Cover
and leave to marinate in the refrigerator for at least
6 hours or overnight, turning once.

❸ Drain the duck, reserving the marinade, and pat the
duck dry on kitchen paper. Heat the oil in a heavy-
based frying pan and fry the duck pieces, skin side
down, for 5 minutes until dark golden. Transfer to a
roasting tin and cook in a preheated oven, 180°C
(350°F), Gas Mark 4, for about 30 minutes or until
tender. Transfer the duck to a warm dish and drain off
all the fat from the tin.

❹ Strain the reserved marinade into the tin and bring it
to the boil. Reduce the heat and stir in the chocolate
to make a smooth, glossy sauce. Spoon over the duck
on warmed serving plates.

Festive game pie

Perfect for making ahead, this pie will sit well in the refrigerator overnight, ready to pop in the oven the next day. Serve any excess stock in a serving jug.

Preparation time 45 minutes, plus cooling

Cooking time about 1½ hours

Serves 8

450 g (14½ oz) sausagemeat

2 onions, finely chopped

2 teaspoons chopped thyme

75 g (3 oz) butter

400 g (13 oz) lean turkey, diced

4 pigeon breasts, sliced

500 g (1 lb) diced pheasant

2 celery sticks, thinly sliced

3 garlic cloves, crushed

3 tablespoons plain flour

900 ml (1½ pints) Chicken Stock (see page 18)

200 g (7 oz) cooked peeled chestnuts

400 g (13 oz) shortcrust pastry (see page 46), thawed if frozen

beaten egg, to glaze

1 Mix the sausagemeat with 1 onion and a little thyme and shape it into 18 small balls.

2 Melt 25 g (1 oz) butter in a frying pan and fry the meatballs until golden. Drain. Fry all the meats, in batches, until golden, adding more butter if needed. Drain.

3 Melt the rest of the butter in the pan and fry the remaining onion, celery and garlic. Blend in the flour, add the stock and bring to the boil. Cook for 4–5 minutes.

4 Mix all the meats and chestnuts in a 2 litre (3½ pint) pie dish and pour over enough of the liquid to come to within 2 cm (¾ inch) of the rim. Leave to cool.

5 Roll out the pastry on a lightly floured surface to make a cover for the dish (see page 43). Put the pastry lid in place, brush with beaten egg and bake in a preheated oven, 190°C (375°F), Gas Mark 5, for 1 hour, covering with foil if the pastry begins to get too brown.

Quails with lime, chilli and ginger

This quick and easy supper dish is great for preparing several hours (or even up to a day) in advance so it's ready to pop into the oven for a quick roasting.

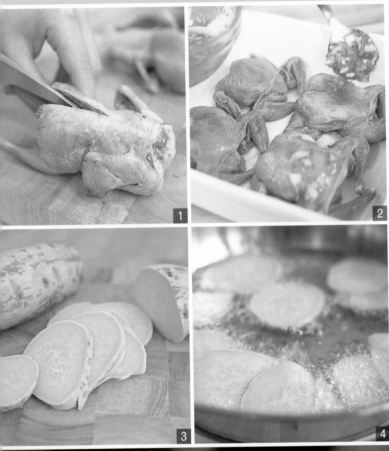

Preparation time 15 minutes, plus marinating
Cooking time 20 minutes
Serves 2

4 quails
1 red chilli, deseeded and finely chopped
2 garlic cloves, crushed
15 g (½ oz) fresh root ginger, grated
2 tablespoons clear honey
1 tablespoon light muscovado sugar
juice of 1 lime
2 tablespoons vegetable oil, plus extra for frying
500 g (1 lb) slender sweet potatoes, scrubbed
salt and pepper

1. Use kitchen scissors or shears to cut off the wing tips from the quails, then cut through each bird, either side of the backbone. Discard the backbone and flatten each bird. Place them in a shallow, ovenproof dish into which they fit quite snugly.

2. Mix the chilli with the garlic, ginger, honey, sugar, lime juice, seasoning and 2 tablespoons oil. Pour the mixture over the quails, cover with clingfilm and chill until ready to cook.

3. Uncover the quails and roast in a preheated oven, 200°C (400°F), Gas Mark 6, for 20 minutes until the quails are just beginning to brown. Meanwhile, slice the sweet potatoes as thinly as possible.

4. Pour oil to a depth of 2 cm (¾ inch) into a large, heavy-based frying pan and heat until a slice of potato sizzles on the surface. Fry the potatoes in 2 batches until golden. Drain on kitchen paper.

5. Transfer the quails and chips to warm serving plates and spoon over the juices.

Tea-smoked partridge

Fragrant leaf tea makes a subtly flavoured smoking medium for lighter game meats as well as more everyday meats, such as chicken or guinea fowl.

Preparation time 20 minutes
Cooking time 35 minutes
Serves 4

8 partridge breasts, skinned
3 tablespoons strong tea leaves, such as jasmine
3 tablespoons demerara sugar
200 g (7 oz) fragrant rice, plus 4 tablespoons
2 tablespoons sesame oil
2 tablespoons clear honey
2 tablespoons soy sauce
5 tablespoons seasoned rice vinegar
100 g (3½ oz) oyster mushrooms
40 g (1½ oz) fresh root ginger, grated
1 tablespoon sesame seeds, toasted
1 bunch of spring onions, finely shredded
3 tablespoons Thai or green basil leaves

① Score the partridge with a sharp knife. Line the base and halfway up the sides of a wok with foil. Add the tea leaves, sugar and 4 tablespoons rice. Heat the wok until the mixture starts to smoke.

② Fit the rack into the wok and lay the partridge on top. Brush with 1 tablespoon oil, cover and smoke for 20 minutes.

③ Mix the remaining oil with the honey, soy sauce and 3 tablespoons vinegar in a small ovenproof dish. Stir in the mushrooms. Add the partridge breasts, turning them in the juices, and cook in a preheated oven, 180°C (350°F), Gas Mark 4, for 15 minutes or until tender.

④ Meanwhile, cook the rice. Drain and toss with the ginger, sesame seeds, spring onions, basil and remaining vinegar. Spoon on to serving plates, top with the partridge and mushrooms and spoon over the juices.

Turkey with creole sauce

Frying turkey pieces in a crisp, spicy crumb coat keeps the meat moist and succulent. The pineapple and pepper sauce add a delicious contrast in both texture and flavour.

Preparation time 25 minutes
Cooking time 25 minutes
Serves 4

500 g (1 lb) piece turkey breast fillet
½ teaspoon paprika
1 tablespoon plain flour
1 egg, beaten
100 g (3½ oz) breadcrumbs
vegetable oil, for frying
salt

Creole sauce
2 tablespoons vegetable oil
1 onion, chopped
2 red peppers, deseeded and chopped
2 garlic cloves, crushed
500 g (1 lb) tomatoes, skinned (see page 17) and chopped
1 small, sweet pineapple, skinned, cored and chopped
2 teaspoons Tabasco sauce
1–2 teaspoons caster sugar (optional)

❶ Cut the turkey across the grain into 1 cm (½ inch) thick strips. Mix together the paprika, flour and a little salt and coat the turkey in the mixture.

❷ Dip the turkey in the beaten egg and then in the breadcrumbs until coated.

❸ Make the sauce. Heat the oil in a large frying pan and gently fry the onion and peppers for 5–8 minutes or until softened. Add the garlic, tomatoes, pineapple, Tabasco sauce and a little salt to the pan and cook gently for about 10 minutes, stirring frequently, until pulpy. Add a little sugar to the sauce if the pineapple isn't very sweet.

❹ Put oil to a depth of 1 cm (½ inch) in a pan and heat it until a few breadcrumbs gently sizzle. Fry the turkey pieces in the oil until golden, turning once. Drain and serve with the sauce.

Satay sauce

This sauce is deliciously rich, spicy and peanutty. It is generally used as a main meal accompaniment, but it's also good as a dipping sauce for small pieces of skewered chicken, pork or fish.

Preparation time 10 minutes
Cooking time 7 minutes
Serves 4–6

1 lemon grass stalk
1 small onion, chopped
2 garlic cloves, chopped
1 teaspoon shrimp paste or Thai fish sauce
1 teaspoon tamarind paste
1 hot red chilli, deseeded and chopped
2 tablespoons water
1 tablespoon light muscovado sugar
200 ml (7 fl oz) coconut milk
175 g (6 oz) smooth or crunchy peanut butter
1 tablespoon soy sauce

1 Trim the ends from the lemon grass and remove any coarse or damaged outer leaves. Cut the lemon grass into thin slices.

2 Put the lemon grass, onion, garlic, shrimp paste or fish sauce, tamarind paste and chilli into a food processor or blender. Add the water and sugar and blend to a paste, scraping down the mixture from the sides of the bowl if necessary.

3 Transfer the mixture to a saucepan with the coconut milk. Bring almost to the boil (watching closely so that the coconut milk does not boil over), then reduce the heat and simmer gently for 5 minutes.

4 Add the peanut butter and soy sauce and cook gently for 2 minutes or until the sauce is heated through and thickened. Check the seasoning, adding a dash more soy sauce, if liked, and more coconut milk if the sauce is too thick. Transfer to a serving bowl and serve warm.

DESSERTS

Blueberries in kirsch

These blueberries are deliciously indulgent to eat spooned over vanilla ice cream or pancakes and crème fraîche. Alternatively, fold the berries into whipped cream for a special cake filling.

Preparation time 10 minutes, plus standing
Makes 400 g (13 oz)

175 g (6 oz) blueberries, destalked
50 g (2 oz) caster sugar
100 ml (3½ fl oz) kirsch

1 Pick over the blueberries, discarding any very soft ones. Prick each berry with a fork.

2 Layer the berries in a clean, dry jar, sprinkling each layer with some sugar.

3 Pour over the kirsch.

4 Seal tightly and shake once or twice. Leave in a cool place and turn the jar upside down every day for 4 days until the sugar has completely dissolved. Label and leave to mature in a cool, dark place for 3–4 weeks before using or store, unopened, for 6–12 months.

Peppered panna cotta with strawberry sauce

The idea of flavouring fruit dishes with pepper is a traditional one, so don't be put off. Omit the pepper for a milder flavour.

Preparation time 20 minutes, plus setting
Cooking time 3 minutes
Serves 6

1 teaspoon pink peppercorns in brine
1 teaspoon powdered gelatine
250 g (8 oz) mascarpone cheese
300 ml (½ pint) double cream
150 g (5 oz) white chocolate, chopped
300 g (10 oz) strawberries
2–3 tablespoons icing sugar

To decorate
piped chocolate scribbles (see page 56)
fresh strawberries

❶ Rinse and dry the peppercorns. Use a pestle and mortar to crush them until fairly finely ground. Sprinkle the gelatine over 2 tablespoons water in a small bowl and leave to stand for 5 minutes. Lightly oil 6 dariole moulds, each holding 125 ml (4 fl oz).

❷ Put the mascarpone in a medium-sized saucepan with the cream and crushed peppercorns and bring just to the boil, stirring until smooth. Remove from the heat and add the gelatine. Stir for about 1 minute or until dissolved, then tip in the chocolate. Leave until melted.

❸ Transfer the mixture to a jug, then pour it into the moulds, stirring between each pour to distribute the peppercorns evenly. Chill for several hours or overnight until set.

❹ Blend the strawberries in a food processor with a little icing sugar and 1 tablespoon water until smooth. Test for sweetness, adding more sugar if necessary.

❺ Loosen the edges of the moulds with a knife and shake them out on to plates. Spoon the sauce around and decorate with piped chocolate scribbles and strawberries.

Sunken torte with orange liqueur cream

This chocolate cake rises during baking only to sink again as it cools. Don't be put off: the moist density of the mixture makes it utterly delicious.

Preparation time 20 minutes
Cooking time 30 minutes
Serves 8

250 g (8 oz) plain chocolate, chopped
125 g (4 oz) unsalted butter
1 teaspoon vanilla extract
6 medium eggs, separated
125 g (4 oz) light muscovado sugar
250 ml (8 fl oz) Greek yogurt
finely grated rind and juice of ½ orange
2 tablespoons orange liqueur
2 tablespoons icing sugar
chocolate curls (see page 57), to decorate

1 Grease and line a 23 cm (9 inch) spring-form or loose-based cake tin with greaseproof paper, then grease the paper. Melt the chocolate with the butter in a small bowl and stir in the vanilla extract.

2 Whisk the egg yolks with 100 g (3½ oz) sugar in a large bowl for 3–4 minutes until the mixture leaves a trail when the whisk is lifted from the bowl. Fold in the chocolate mixture.

3 Whisk the egg whites in a completely clean bowl until peaking. Gradually whisk in the remaining sugar. Fold a quarter of the whisked whites into the chocolate mixture to lighten it, then fold in the remainder.

4 Turn into the tin and bake in a preheated oven, 160°C (325°F), Gas Mark 3, for 30 minutes or until well risen and springy.

5 Meanwhile, beat together the yogurt, orange rind and juice, liqueur and icing sugar until smooth, then chill. Leave the cake to cool in the tin for 10 minutes before serving with the orange cream and chocolate curls.

Flaked lime and coconut ice cream

A fabulous 'make-ahead' special dessert of sweet, tangy ice cream, interleaved with flaky bites of dark chocolate.

Preparation time 30 minutes, plus freezing
Cooking time 3 minutes
Serves 8

6 egg yolks
175 g (6 oz) caster sugar
2 teaspoons cornflour
2 x 400 ml (14 fl oz) cans coconut milk
finely grated rind and juice of 4 limes
200 g (7 oz) plain chocolate, chopped
450 ml (¾ pint) double or whipping cream
cocoa powder, for dusting

❶ Whisk together the egg yolks, sugar and cornflour. Bring the coconut milk almost to the boil in a saucepan and pour it over the egg mixture, whisking well. Return the custard to the pan and cook gently, stirring, until slightly thickened. Transfer to a bowl, cover with a circle of greaseproof paper and leave to cool. Stir in the lime rind and juice.

❷ Melt the chocolate (see page 56). Cut 2 lengths of nonstick baking paper, each 46 x 33 cm (18 x 13 inches). Spoon half the chocolate on to each sheet, spreading it as thinly as possible. Leave until it is beginning to set, then chill, bending the sheets if necessary.

❸ Whip the cream until it just holds its shape. Stir into the custard and freeze for 4–6 hours until softly set. Alternatively, if you have an ice cream maker, stir the cream into the custard and churn until softly set.

❹ Peel the chocolate from the paper, breaking it into flakes. Reserve a handful. Spoon a quarter of the ice cream into a freezer-proof dish and scatter with one-third of the chocolate. Repeat the layering and arrange the reserved flakes on top. Freeze until firm and serve dusted with cocoa powder.

Plum and lemon tart

The sweet, juicy plums and sharp, fresh lemon custard make a delicious combination in this recipe. Serve the tart warm or cold with lightly whipped cream.

Preparation time 30 minutes, plus chilling

Cooking time 40–45 minutes

Serves 6–8

175 g (6 oz) pâte sucrée
(see page 47)

50 g (2 oz) butter, at room temperature

50 g (2 oz) caster sugar

50 g (2 oz) semolina

grated rind of 1 lemon

1 egg, beaten

750 g (1½ lb) ripe plums, halved and stoned

4 tablespoons apricot jam

whipped cream, to serve

1 Roll out the pastry on a lightly floured surface and line a 23 cm (9 inch) tart tin. Prick the pastry base with a fork, then chill for 30 minutes.

2 Make the filling. Beat together the butter and sugar in a bowl until light and fluffy. Beat in the semolina, lemon rind and egg, then spread the mixture over the pastry base.

3 Arrange the plum halves over the top of the pastry base, cut sides down. Bake the tart in a preheated oven, 190°C (375°F), Gas Mark 5, for 40–45 minutes or until the pastry is browned and the filling is golden and set.

4 Warm the jam in a small saucepan, then press it through a sieve into a bowl or jug. Brush the apricot glaze over the tart. Serve the whipped cream separately.

French apple flan

For a special occasion, sprinkle a few drops of Calvados (the brandy made from distilled cider) over the apple slices when you arrange them in the tart.

Preparation time 30 minutes, plus chilling
Cooking time 40–45 minutes
Serves 8

250 g (8 oz) pâte sucrée (see page 47)
750 g (1½ lb) eating apples
3 tablespoons lemon juice
4 tablespoons warmed, sieved apricot jam
175 ml (6 fl oz) single cream
2 eggs, beaten
50 g (2 oz) caster sugar

❶ Roll out the pastry on a lightly floured surface and line a 25 cm (10 inch) tart tin. Prick the pastry base with a fork, then chill for 30 minutes.

❷ Peel and core the apples. Slice them thinly into a bowl and toss with the lemon juice. Drain the apples and arrange them in concentric circles over the base of the pastry case.

❸ Brush the apricot jam over the apple slices and bake the tart in a preheated oven, 220°C (425°F), Gas Mark 7, for 10 minutes. Reduce the oven temperature to 190°C (375°F), Gas Mark 5.

❹ Whisk the cream, eggs and sugar in a bowl. Pour the mixture carefully over the apples. Return the flan to the oven and bake for 30–35 minutes or until the pastry is golden and the filling is cooked. Serve warm.

Baked custard tart

Fresh nutmeg has a far superior flavour to the ready-grated spice. Keep nutmegs in an airtight container so that the aroma and flavour are not dissipated.

Preparation time 20 minutes, plus chilling
Cooking time about 1 hour 10 minutes
Serves 6

175 g (6 oz) shortcrust pastry (see page 46), thawed if frozen
4 eggs
25 g (1 oz) caster sugar
½ teaspoon vanilla essence
450 ml (¾ pint) milk
grated nutmeg

1 Roll out the pastry on a lightly floured surface and line a 20 cm (8 inch) tart tin. Chill for 30 minutes, then bake blind (see page 44) in a preheated oven, 200°C (400°F), Gas Mark 6, for 15 minutes. Remove the paper and beans or foil and return to the oven for a further 5 minutes. Reduce the oven temperature to 160°C (325°F), Gas Mark 3.

2 Lightly whisk the eggs with the sugar and vanilla essence in a bowl. Heat the milk until warm and whisk into the beaten egg mixture.

3 Strain the custard into the pastry case.

4 Sprinkle the tart with grated nutmeg. Bake in the oven for 45–50 minutes or until the custard is set and lightly browned. Serve warm or cold.

Chocolate and passion fruit roulade

Chocolate roulades have a soft, squidgy texture and a sugary crust, which cracks when it is rolled up so it looks craggy, moist and appealing.

Preparation time 20 minutes, plus cooling

Cooking time 20 minutes

Serves 8

175 g (6 oz) plain chocolate, chopped

5 eggs, separated

125 g (4 oz) caster sugar, plus extra to sprinkle

4 passion fruit, halved and scooped out

4 tablespoons orange curd

225 ml (7½ fl oz) double cream

chocolate curls (see page 57), to decorate

1 Grease and line a 33 x 23 cm (13 x 9 inch) Swiss roll tin with greaseproof paper, then grease the paper. Melt the chocolate in a small bowl (see page 56). Beat together the yolks and sugar for 3–4 minutes or until thickened and pale.

2 Using a metal spoon, fold the beaten yolks and sugar mixture into the melted chocolate.

3 Whisk the egg whites in a clean bowl until peaking but not stiff. Fold about a quarter of the whisked whites into the chocolate mixture to lighten it, then fold in the remainder. Spread the mixture gently into the corners of the tin.

4 Bake in a preheated oven, 180°C (350°F), Gas Mark 4, for about 20 minutes or until risen and just firm. Invert the roulade on to a sheet of greaseproof paper sprinkled with caster sugar and peel away the lining paper. Cover and leave to cool. Add the passion fruit pulp to the orange curd and mix. Lightly whip the cream. Spread the cream just to the edges of the roulade. Spoon the passion fruit mixture over the top, then roll up the roulade, using the paper.

5 Turn on to a plate, join underneath, and scatter with chocolate curls.

Blueberry pie

Fresh blueberries have a fairly short season, but frozen berries
are available and can be used equally successfully in this pie.
The flavour of this pretty fruit is intensified by cooking.

Preparation time 25 minutes, plus chilling
Cooking time 30–35 minutes
Serves 6

375 g (12 oz) pâte sucrée (see page 47)
250 g (8 oz) fresh or frozen blueberries, thawed if frozen
25 g (1 oz) sugar
milk, to glaze
50 g (2 oz) flaked almonds, to decorate
cream or crème fraîche, to serve

❶ Roll out about two-thirds of the pastry on a lightly
floured surface and line a 23 cm (9 inch) tart tin. Chill
for 30 minutes. Spread the blueberries evenly over the
pastry case and sprinkle with the sugar.

❷ Roll out the remaining pastry and cut it into thin strips.

❸ Brush the rim of the tart with water and arrange the
pastry strips in a lattice pattern over the top.

❹ Brush the pastry with a little milk and sprinkle the
flaked almonds over the surface.

❺ Bake in a preheated oven, 190°C (375°F), Gas Mark 5,
for 30–35 minutes or until the pastry is golden and the
blueberries are tender. Serve warm or cold with cream
or crème fraîche.

Chocolate fig tatin

Take a short cut to a delicious tarte tatin by using bought puff pastry, sandwiched with chocolaty layers. Serve warm topped with melting ice cream or crème fraîche.

Preparation time 20 minutes
Cooking time 35 minutes
Serves 6

100 g (3½ oz) plain chocolate, grated
1 teaspoon ground mixed spice
75 g (3 oz) caster sugar, plus 2 tablespoons
500 g (1 lb) puff pastry (see page 48), thawed if frozen
75 g (3 oz) unsalted butter, plus extra for greasing
10 fresh figs, quartered
1 tablespoon lemon juice
vanilla ice cream or crème fraîche, to serve

❶ Mix together the chocolate, spice and 2 tablespoons sugar. Cut the pastry into 3 evenly sized pieces and roll out each piece on a lightly floured surface to a circle 25 cm (10 inches) across, using a plate or inverted bowl as a guide.

❷ Scatter 2 rounds to within 2 cm (¾ inch) of the edges with the grated chocolate mixture. Stack the pastry layers so that the chocolate is sandwiched in 2 layers. Press the pastry down firmly around the edges.

❸ Lightly butter the sides of a shallow 23 cm (9 inch) round baking tin, 4 cm (1½ inches) deep. (Don't use a loose-based tin.) Melt the butter in a frying pan. Add the sugar and heat gently until dissolved. Add the figs and cook for 3 minutes or until lightly coloured and the syrup begins to turn golden. Add the lemon juice.

❹ Tip the figs into the tin, spreading them in an even layer. Lay the pastry over the figs, tucking the dough down inside the edges of the tin. Bake in a preheated oven, 200°C (400°F), Gas Mark 6, for 30 minutes until well risen and golden. Leave for 5 minutes, then loosen the edges and invert on to a serving plate.

Lemon meringue pie

For best results, whisk the egg whites in a clean, dry and grease-free bowl. Some cooks like to add a pinch of salt or a few drops of lemon juice to help the foam keep its shape.

Preparation time 35 minutes, plus chilling

Cooking time 50 minutes

Serves 6

175 g (6 oz) pâte sucrée (see page 47)

25 g (1 oz) cornflour

100 g (3½ oz) caster sugar

grated rind of 2 lemons

juice of 1 lemon

25 g (1 oz) butter, diced

2 egg yolks

Meringue

3 egg whites

175 g (6 oz) caster sugar

1 Roll out the pastry on a lightly floured surface and line a 20 cm (8 inch) tart tin. Chill for 30 minutes, then bake blind (see page 44) in a preheated oven, 200°C (400°F), Gas Mark 6, for 15 minutes. Remove the paper and beans or foil and return to the oven for a further 5 minutes. Leave the oven on. Meanwhile, mix the cornflour and caster sugar in a saucepan. Stir in 150 ml (¼ pint) water and the lemon rind and juice until well blended. Bring to the boil, stirring, until the sauce is thickened and smooth.

2 Take it off the heat and stir in the butter. Leave to cool slightly. Whisk the egg yolks in a bowl. Whisk in 2 tablespoons of the sauce and then return all the mixture to the pan. Cook gently until the sauce has thickened further.

3 Pour the lemon sauce into the pastry case. Return to the oven for 15 minutes until the filling has set. Whisk the egg whites until stiff and dry. Whisk in 1 tablespoon of sugar, then fold in the rest.

4 Spread the meringue mixture so that it completely covers the filling. Return the pie to the oven for 10 minutes or until golden. Serve warm or cold.

Zucotto

To form a good domed shape for this classic Italian speciality, use a mixing bowl with a rounded base. Serve the cake cut into wedges with morning or after-dinner coffee.

Preparation time 25 minutes, plus chilling
Serves 6–8

350 g (11½ oz) bought or homemade chocolate sponge cake, thinly sliced

350 ml (12 fl oz) double cream

4 tablespoons maraschino liqueur or brandy

40 g (1½ oz) icing sugar, plus extra for dusting

75 g (3 oz) plain chocolate, chopped

50 g (2 oz) whole sweet almonds, toasted and chopped

50 g (2 oz) unblanched hazelnuts, toasted and chopped

75 g (3 oz) natural glacé cherries, halved

cocoa powder, for dusting

1 Line a 1.8 litre (3 pint) bowl with clingfilm. Use about two-thirds of the cake slices to line the bowl in a single layer, cutting the pieces to fit neatly together. The lining should come about two-thirds of the way up the sides of the bowl.

2 Put the cream, liqueur or brandy and icing sugar in a bowl and whisk until just peaking. Stir in the chocolate, nuts and cherries.

3 Spoon the mixture into the cake-lined bowl, spreading it in an even layer.

4 Use the remaining cake and any excess cake that is lining the bowl to cover the top of the filling. Cover the bowl with clingfilm and chill overnight.

5 Invert the cake on to a plate and peel away the clingfilm. Cut 4 wedge-shaped templates from paper. Dust the cake with icing sugar and lay the templates over the top with their points meeting in the centre to make a sunburst pattern. Dust between the paper with cocoa powder, then carefully lift away the paper.

Linzertorte

This delicious tart takes its name from the Austrian town of Linz. It is distinguished by the pastry, which is made with ground almonds.

Preparation time 25 minutes
Cooking time 25–30 minutes
Serves 6

150 g (5 oz) plain flour
½ teaspoon ground cinnamon
75 g (3 oz) unsalted butter, diced
50 g (2 oz) sugar
50 g (2 oz) ground almonds
2 teaspoons finely grated lemon rind
2 large egg yolks
about 1 tablespoon lemon juice
325 g (11 oz) raspberry jam
icing sugar, to decorate

1 Sift the flour and cinnamon into a bowl. Rub in the butter until the mixture resembles fine breadcrumbs. Add the sugar, almonds and lemon rind.

2 Bind the mixture with the egg yolks and enough lemon juice to make a stiff dough. Turn out the dough on to a floured surface and knead lightly.

3 Roll out two-thirds of the dough and line a greased 18–20 cm (7–8 inch) fluted flan ring placed on a baking sheet. Make sure the dough is evenly rolled out, press it to the shape of the ring and trim off the excess. Fill the tart with the raspberry jam.

4 Roll out the reserved dough and the trimmings and cut it into long strips with a pastry wheel or knife. Use these to make a lattice over the jam.

5 Bake the tart in a preheated oven, 190°C (375°F), Gas Mark 5, for 25–30 minutes until golden-brown. Leave to cool, then remove the flan ring. Sprinkle icing sugar over the top just before serving.

Chocolate velvet pie

This chocolate shortbread base is an interesting variation on traditional plain shortbread. Swirls of whipped double cream would make a decadent finishing touch.

Preparation time 35 minutes, plus chilling
Cooking time 22 minutes
Serves 10

Shortbread
175 g (6 oz) plain flour
2 teaspoons cocoa powder
125 g (4 oz) unsalted butter, diced
25 g (1 oz) caster sugar

Filling
4 teaspoons powdered gelatine
125 g (4 oz) caster sugar
3 egg yolks
1 tablespoon cornflour
600 ml (1 pint) milk
2 tablespoons finely ground espresso coffee
50 g (2 oz) plain chocolate, chopped
chocolate shavings (see page 57), to decorate

1 Make the shortbread. Sift the flour and cocoa powder together, then rub in the butter. Add the sugar and mix to a dough.

2 Press evenly over the base and sides of a lightly buttered, deep 20 cm (8 inch) fluted tart tin. Bake for 20 minutes in a preheated oven, 180°C (350°F), Gas Mark 4, then leave to cool.

3 Soak the gelatine in 3 tablespoons cold water. Whisk together the sugar, egg yolks, cornflour and 2 tablespoons milk. Bring the rest of the milk to the boil with the coffee powder. Whisk it into the egg mixture.

4 Return the mixture to the saucepan and heat gently, stirring, until it thickens. Remove from the heat and beat in the gelatine until dissolved. Add the chocolate and stir until it has melted. Cool slightly then pour the mixture into the tart case. Chill for several hours. Transfer the pie to a plate and scatter generously with chocolate shavings.

Cheesecake tart with Grand Marnier berries

Soaking the dried berries in liqueur not only plumps them up but also ensures that the orange flavour permeates the filling.

Preparation time 15 minutes, plus chilling
Cooking time about 1 hour
Serves 8

175 g (6 oz) dried mixed berries and cherries
5 tablespoons Grand Marnier
2 tablespoons clear honey
grated rind of 1 lemon
200 g (7 oz) pâte sucrée (see page 47)
250 g (8 oz) ricotta cheese
200 g (7 oz) cream cheese
100 g (3½ oz) caster sugar
3 whole eggs, plus 1 yolk
25 g (1 oz) flaked almonds
crème fraîche, to serve

1 Put the dried fruit in a small pan with the Grand Marnier, honey and lemon rind. Warm over a low heat until the liquid starts to boil. Remove from the heat, cover and leave until cold.

2 Roll out the pastry on a lightly floured surface and line a 23 cm (9 inch) tart tin. Leave to chill for 30 minutes, then trim away the excess pastry. Bake blind (see page 44) in a preheated oven, 180°C (350°F), Gas Mark 4, for 20 minutes. Remove the paper and beans or foil and return the tart to the oven for a further 5 minutes. Leave the oven on.

3 Beat together the two cheeses, sugar and eggs to make a smooth custard.

4 Stir in half the dried fruit mixture and pour into the pastry case. Bake for 35 minutes until the tart is firm to the touch and golden on top.

5 Spoon the remaining dried fruit mixture over the top and top with the flaked almonds. Leave to cool and serve with crème fraîche and a glass of Grand Marnier.

Chocolate Amaretto jellies

Try these delicious 'grown-up' jellies, laced with almond liqueur.
They're set in little jelly moulds, but you could use small metal
pudding moulds instead.

   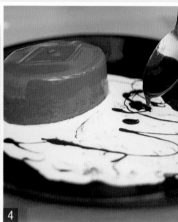

Preparation time 15 minutes,
plus setting

Cooking time 5 minutes

Serves 8

1 tablespoon powdered gelatine

300 g (10 oz) plain chocolate,
chopped

150 ml (¼ pint) Amaretto liqueur

450 ml (¾ pint) milk

100 ml (3½ fl oz) double cream

1 quantity Glossy Chocolate Sauce
(see page 58)

① Sprinkle the gelatine over 3 tablespoons water in a small bowl and leave
to soak for 5 minutes. Melt the chocolate in a large bowl (see page 56) with
the liqueur, stirring frequently until smooth.

② Bring the milk just to the boil and remove from the heat.

③ Pour the warm milk over the chocolate, whisking well until completely
combined and smooth. Add the soaked gelatine and stir for 1 minute
until dissolved. Spoon the mixture into 8 individual moulds, each holding
125–150 ml (4–5 fl oz), and leave to cool. Chill for at least 6 hours, preferably
overnight, until just firm.

④ Half-fill a small bowl with very hot water and dip a mould up to the rim in
the water for 2 seconds. Invert on to a serving plate and, gripping both
plate and mould, shake the jelly on to the plate. Lift away the mould.
Repeat with the other jellies. Pour a little cream around each jelly, then
drizzle a tablespoonful of sauce through it. Lightly swirl the sauce into the
cream to decorate.

Peach and raspberry tartlets

These tempting tartlets are simple to make. The tartlet can be cooked several hours ahead, but should be filled just before eating so that the pastry does not go soft.

Preparation time 15 minutes
Cooking time 8–10 minutes
Serves 4

15 g (½ oz) butter, melted
4 sheets of filo pastry, each about 25 cm (10 inches) square
125 ml (4 fl oz) double cream
1 tablespoon soft brown sugar
2 peaches, halved, stoned and diced
50 g (2 oz) raspberries
icing sugar, to dust

❶ Grease 4 deep muffin tins with the melted butter. Cut each sheet of filo pastry into 4 equal squares and use these to line each muffin tin, arranging the pieces at slightly different angles. Press them down well, tucking the pastry into the tin neatly.

❷ Bake the filo cases in a preheated oven, 190°C (375°F), Gas Mark 5, for 8–10 minutes or until golden. Carefully remove the cases from the tins and leave them to cool on a wire rack.

❸ Pour the cream into a bowl and add the sugar. Whip lightly until it holds its shape.

❹ Spoon the cream into the tartlet cases and top with the peaches and raspberries. Dust with icing sugar and serve immediately.

Baked fig tarts

Figs are an ancient fruit, cultivated by the ancient Egyptians as long ago as 1,900 BC. If you prefer, you can use plums instead of figs in this recipe.

Preparation time 20 minutes, plus chilling
Cooking time 25–40 minutes
Serves 6

400 g (13 oz) pâte sucrée (see page 47)
50 g (2 oz) butter
125 g (4 oz) caster sugar
3 medium eggs, beaten
125 g (4 oz) ground almonds
5 tablespoons plum jam
6 figs
1 vanilla pod, split
150 ml (¼ pint) orange juice
icing sugar, for dusting
thick cream or crème fraîche, to serve

1 Roll out the pastry and line a 20 cm (8 inch) loose-based tart tin or 4 individual 10 cm (4 inch) loose-based tart tins. Chill for 30 minutes, then bake the pastry blind (see page 44) in a preheated oven, 200°C (400°F), Gas Mark 6, for 10 minutes. Remove the paper and beans or foil and return to the oven for a further 5 minutes. Leave the oven on.

2 Cream the butter with 75 g (3 oz) sugar and gradually add the beaten eggs. Beat well and then add the ground almonds.

3 Spread the jam over the bottom of the pastry and then spoon the almond mixture over the top. Arrange the figs on top. Bake in the oven for 10–12 minutes for individual tarts or 20 minutes for a large one or until the sponge has risen and is firm to the touch.

4 Meanwhile, put the remaining sugar in a saucepan with the vanilla pod and orange juice and heat gently to dissolve the sugar, then boil to reduce. Brush over the figs and leave to cool. Dust with icing sugar and serve with thick cream or crème fraîche.

Praline choux tart

Choux pastry doesn't take long to make, but the results always look spectacular. Make this tart for a special occasion. Fresh ripe strawberries are the finishing touch.

Preparation time 30 minutes
Cooking time 30 minutes
Serves 6

75 g (3 oz) choux pastry (see page 49)
150 g (5 oz) whole almonds, lightly toasted and roughly chopped
150 g (5 oz) caster sugar
175 g (6 oz) mascarpone cheese
50 ml (2 fl oz) double cream
1 tablespoon icing sugar
fresh berries, to decorate (optional)

❶ Spoon just over one-third of the pastry on to a baking sheet and use the back of a spoon to spread it out into a 22 cm (8½ inch) disc.

❷ Space small spoonfuls of the remaining mixture well apart on another baking sheet. Bake in a preheated oven, 200°C (400°F), Gas Mark 6, for 20 minutes until golden. Leave the oven on. Pierce each bun once and the base a few times to let the steam escape. Return to the oven for 5 minutes to dry. If the base is not dry enough give it a further 5 minutes. Leave the pastry on a wire rack to cool.

❸ Put the almonds on a lightly greased piece of foil. Melt the sugar with 3 tablespoons water over a medium heat until it is a rich golden colour. Pour over the almonds and leave to cool. Break the praline into pieces. Crush half in a plastic bag with a rolling pin.

❹ Whisk the mascarpone, cream and crushed praline until thickened. Attach the buns around the sides of the pastry base with a little cream and spoon the rest into the centre of the tart.

❺ Dust with icing sugar and decorate the tart with the remaining praline pieces and fresh berries.

Crème anglaise

Smooth, creamy and comforting, custard is always a great favourite and well worth the effort of making from scratch to add the finishing touch to a baked dessert.

Preparation time 10 minutes, plus infusing
Cooking time 10–15 minutes
Serves 6

1 vanilla pod, split lengthways
300 ml (½ pint) full-cream milk
300 ml (½ pint) single cream
6 egg yolks
25 g (1 oz) caster sugar

❶ Put the vanilla pod into a heavy-based saucepan with the milk and cream and bring slowly to the boil. Remove from the heat and leave to infuse for 15 minutes.

❷ Whisk together the egg yolks and sugar in a bowl with a balloon whisk until thick and pale. Lift the vanilla pod out of the pan and scrape the seeds into the pan.

❸ Pour the milk over the creamed mixture, whisking well.

❹ Return the mixture to the cleaned pan and cook over a medium heat, stirring constantly with a wooden spoon, until the sauce thickly coats the back of the spoon. This will take 5–10 minutes, but don't be tempted to raise the heat or the custard might curdle. Serve warm.

Red fruit coulis

Summer fruits, blended and strained to a smooth and colourful purée, make a useful sauce for setting off all sorts of summery desserts, either flooding the plate or drizzled around the edge.

Preparation time 10 minutes, plus cooling
Serves 6–8

3 tablespoons caster sugar

500 g (1 lb) ripe summer fruits, such as strawberries, raspberries and redcurrants

2–3 teaspoons lemon juice

❶ Put the sugar into a small jug and make it up to 50 ml (3½ fl oz) with boiling water. Stir until the sugar dissolves and leave to cool.

❷ Remove the redcurrants, if using, from their stalks by running them through the tines of a fork. Place all the fruits in a food processor or blender and blend to a smooth purée, scraping the mixture down from the sides of the bowl if necessary. Blend in the cooled sugar syrup.

❸ Pour the sauce into a sieve set over a bowl. Press the purée with the back of a large metal spoon to squeeze out all the juice.

❹ Stir in enough lemon juice to make the sauce slightly tangy, then transfer it to a jug. To serve, pour a little coulis on to each serving plate and gently tilt the plate so it is covered in an even layer. Alternatively, use a tablespoon to drizzle the sauce in a ribbon around the edges.

Cinnamon sabayon

Sweet, foamy sabayon can be served as a dessert on its own or, more frequently, as a light and airy sauce. It needs to be made just before serving as it will slowly collapse.

Preparation time 5 minutes
Cooking time 10 minutes, plus standing
Serves 5–6

¼ teaspoon ground cinnamon
4 tablespoons coffee liqueur
4 egg yolks
25 g (1 oz) caster sugar

1 Blend the cinnamon with 4 tablespoons cold water in a large, heatproof bowl.

2 Add the coffee liqueur, egg yolks and sugar.

3 Set the bowl over a saucepan of gently simmering water. Make sure the base of the bowl does not come in contact with the water or the sauce will overheat.

4 Use a balloon whisk or a hand-held electric whisk to beat the ingredients for about 5 minutes until they are light and aerated and the whisk leaves a trail when lifted from the mixture.

5 If you are serving the sauce hot, serve it immediately. If it is to be served cold, remove the bowl from the heat and whisk for a further 2–3 minutes, then leave it to stand for 10 minutes.

CAKES
AND BAKES

Moist ricotta cake

This cake is delicious with a cup of tea or coffee after a light meal. If you think of it in time, soak the raisins overnight so they've plenty of time to plump up.

Preparation time 20 minutes, plus soaking
Cooking time 40 minutes
Serves 9–10

100 g (3½ oz) raisins
3 tablespoons Marsala
175 g (6 oz) unsalted butter, softened
175 g (6 oz) caster sugar
250 g (8 oz) ricotta cheese
1 teaspoon vanilla extract
3 eggs, separated
150 g (5 oz) self-raising flour
1 teaspoon baking powder
icing sugar, for dusting

1. Grease and base-line an 18 cm (7 inch) square cake tin or a 20 cm (8 inch) round tin. Put the raisins and Marsala in a small bowl and leave them to soak for 30 minutes. Cream together the butter and sugar until light and fluffy. Beat in the ricotta, vanilla extract and egg yolks.

2. Stir in the raisins and any unabsorbed Marsala. In a separate, completely clean bowl whisk the egg whites until peaking.

3. Use a large metal spoon to fold a quarter of the egg whites into the mixture to lighten it, then fold in the remainder.

4. Sift the flour and baking powder into the bowl and fold in until combined. Turn the mixture into the tin and level the surface.

5. Bake in a preheated oven, 180°C (350°F), Gas Mark 4, for 40 minutes or until just firm to the touch. Transfer to a wire rack to cool. Serve dusted with plenty of icing sugar.

Moist cherry and almond cake

This cake is so fabulously moist and almondy that it's difficult to resist. It combines creaming and whisking techniques, which gives it a light, airy texture.

Preparation time 25 minutes
Cooking time 1–1¼ hours
Serves 12

200 g (7 oz) natural glacé cherries
150 g (5 oz) self-raising flour
250 g (8 oz) unsalted butter, softened
250 g (8 oz) golden caster sugar
5 eggs, separated
1 teaspoon almond extract
1 tablespoon lemon juice
150 g (5 oz) ground almonds
15 g (½ oz) flaked almonds

❶ Grease and line a 1.25 kg (2½ lb) loaf tin. Grease the paper. Rinse and dry the cherries, cut them in half and toss them in 1 tablespoon flour.

❷ Cream together the butter and 200 g (7 oz) sugar until the mixture is light and fluffy. Beat in the egg yolks, almond extract and lemon juice. Sift the remaining flour into the bowl and stir in with a large metal spoon.

❸ Whisk the egg whites in a completely clean bowl until peaking. Gradually whisk in the remaining sugar, then fold in the ground almonds.

❹ Fold a quarter of the whisked mixture into the creamed mixture to lighten it, then fold in the remainder, along with half the cherries. Turn the mixture into the tin and level the surface. Scatter the cake with the remaining cherries and flaked almonds.

❺ Bake in a preheated oven, 180°C (350°F), Gas Mark 4, for 1–1¼ hours or until golden and a skewer inserted into the centre comes out clean. Leave to cool in the tin.

Fruity gingerbread

This tray bake is perfect for feeding a crowd and keeps well for several days. It's mildly gingery, rather than spicily hot, so add more ground or stem ginger if you wish.

Preparation time 15 minutes
Cooking time 1 hour
Serves 12–16

450 g (14½ oz) plain flour
2 teaspoons ground ginger
2 teaspoons baking powder
1 teaspoon bicarbonate of soda
175 g (6 oz) lightly salted butter
225 g (7½ oz) molasses sugar
325 g (11 oz) black treacle
300 ml (½ pint) milk
1 egg, beaten
65 g (2½ oz) stem ginger, finely chopped
250 g (8 oz) mixed dried fruit
150 g (5 oz) Glacé Icing (see page 54)

1 Grease and line the base and long sides of a 28 x 23 cm (11 x 9 inch) roasting tin or a similar sized baking tin with a strip of greaseproof paper so it's easy to lift out after baking. Line the ends of the tin and grease the paper. Put the flour, ginger, baking powder and bicarbonate of soda in a bowl.

2 Melt the butter in a small saucepan with the sugar and treacle. Remove from the heat and stir in the milk, then the egg.

3 Stir the mixture into the dry ingredients with the stem ginger and dried fruit and pour into the tin. Level the surface and bake in a preheated oven, 160°C (325°F), Gas Mark 3, for 50–55 minutes or until it is firm to the touch and a skewer inserted into the centre comes out clean. Leave to cool for 10 minutes. Don't worry if it sinks a bit in the middle; gingerbread often does.

4 Lift the cake from the tin, drizzle with the icing and leave to cool.

Baby panettones

We usually see beautifully boxed panettone breads hanging in delicatessens, particularly during the festive season. Once cooled, these mini versions look lovely rewrapped in fresh paper.

Preparation time 25 minutes, plus proving
Cooking time 20–25 minutes
Makes 8 panettones

2 teaspoons easy-blend dried yeast
125 g (4 oz) caster sugar, plus 1 teaspoon
175 ml (6 fl oz) hand-hot milk
700 g (1 lb 6 oz) strong bread flour
4 large eggs, plus 2 yolks
2 teaspoons vanilla extract
finely grated rind of 2 lemons
175 g (6 oz) salted butter, very soft, diced
175 g (6 oz) mixed dried fruit

1. Stir the yeast and 1 teaspoon sugar into the milk in a large, warm bowl and leave for 10 minutes or until frothy. Stir in 100 g (3½ oz) of the flour. Cover with clingfilm and leave for 30 minutes. Meanwhile, grease 8 clean food cans, each holding 400 ml (14 fl oz), and line the sides with greaseproof paper. Grease the paper.

2. Add the eggs and yolks, the remaining flour and sugar and the vanilla extract, lemon rind and butter. Mix well with a round-bladed knife to make a soft dough, adding a little more flour if the dough feels sticky. Turn out on to a lightly floured surface and knead until smooth and elastic. Transfer to a lightly oiled bowl, cover with clingfilm and leave to rise for 2–4 hours or until doubled in size.

3. Knock back the dough (see page 53) and knead in the dried fruit. Cut the dough into 8 pieces and drop them into the cans. Cover and leave to rise until the dough almost reaches the rims.

4. Bake in a preheated oven, 200°C (400°F), Gas Mark 6, for 20–25 minutes or until risen and golden. Leave for 5 minutes, then cool on a wire rack.

Coconut frosted angel cake

Angel cake is as good a way to use up leftover egg whites as a pavlova or meringue. This creamy white, airy sponge is smothered in a contrastingly rich coconut frosting.

Preparation time 30 minutes
Cooking time 25 minutes
Serves 10–12

vegetable oil for brushing
150 g (5 oz) plain flour, plus extra for dusting
8 egg whites
1 teaspoon cream of tartar
225 g (7½ oz) caster sugar
2 teaspoons vanilla extract
toasted coconut shavings, to decorate

Coconut frosting
75 ml (3 fl oz) single cream
50 g (2 oz) creamed coconut, chopped
2–3 teaspoons lemon or lime juice
300 g (10 oz) icing sugar

1 Brush a 1.5 litre (2½ pint) ring tin with oil and coat with flour. Tap out the excess. Beat the egg whites until frothy. Add the cream of tartar and beat until peaking.

2 Gradually beat in the sugar, a tablespoonful at a time, beating well after each addition until the mixture is stiff and glossy. Beat in the vanilla extract with the last of the sugar.

3 Sift the flour into the bowl and gently fold it into the mixture, using a large metal spoon. Turn the mixture into the tin and level the surface. Bake in a preheated oven, 160°C (325°F), Gas Mark 3, for about 25 minutes or until firm to the touch and a skewer inserted into the centre comes out clean.

4 Make the frosting. Gently heat the cream and creamed coconut until the coconut has melted. In a bowl whisk in the lemon or lime juice and icing sugar until thick.

5 Invert the cake on to a wire rack. When cool, loosen the edges of the tin and turn the cake out. Spread with the frosting and scatter with toasted coconut.

Chocolate fudge cake

This is a rich, claggy, chocolate-packed cake with not the faintest hint of dryness. It's great any time, from a midweek indulgence to a holiday or celebratory treat.

Preparation time 25 minutes, plus cooling
Cooking time 20–25 minutes
Serves 12

100 g (3½ oz) cocoa powder
100 g (3½ oz) plain chocolate, chopped
200 g (7 oz) unsalted butter, softened
325 g (11 oz) light muscovado sugar
275 g (9 oz) self-raising flour
½ teaspoon baking powder
3 eggs, beaten

Fudge icing
300 g (10 oz) plain chocolate, chopped
225 g (7½ oz) icing sugar
200 g (7 oz) unsalted butter, softened

1 Grease and base-line 3 sandwich tins, each 20 cm (8 inches) across. (If you have only 2 tins, bake a third of the cake mix afterwards.) Whisk the cocoa powder in a bowl with 300 ml (½ pint) boiling water until smooth. Stir in the chocolate and leave to cool, stirring occasionally.

2 Beat together the butter, sugar, flour, baking powder and eggs until smooth. Beat in the chocolate mixture and spoon equally into the tins. Level the surface and bake in a preheated oven, 180°C (350°F), Gas Mark 4, for 20–25 minutes or until just firm to the touch. Transfer to a wire rack to cool.

3 Make the icing. Melt the chocolate in a small bowl. Remove from the heat and leave to cool slightly. Beat the icing sugar and butter together until creamy, then beat in the chocolate until smooth.

4 Use the icing to sandwich the cake layers on a serving plate. Pile the remainder on top, spreading it evenly with a palette knife over the top and sides.

Liqueur drizzled coffee cake

Use percolator coffee to give this cake its stunning bands of coffee and almond flavouring. If you are using instant coffee, you should reduce the amount to 4 teaspoons.

Preparation time 15 minutes
Cooking time 45 minutes
Serves 8

2 tablespoons espresso coffee powder
50 g (2 oz) ground almonds
50 g (2 oz) dark muscovado sugar
150 g (5 oz) golden caster sugar, plus 1 tablespoon
175 g (6 oz) unsalted butter, softened
3 eggs
200 g (7 oz) self-raising flour
1 teaspoon baking powder
50 g (2 oz) flaked almonds
½ teaspoon ground cinnamon
4 tablespoons coffee liqueur

1. Grease and line the base and sides of an 18 cm (7 inch) spring-form tin or loose-based cake tin. Grease the paper. Mix together the coffee powder, ground almonds and muscovado sugar.

2. Put 150 g (5 oz) caster sugar in a bowl with the butter, eggs, flour and baking powder and beat until smooth and creamy. Spread one-third into the tin and scatter with half the coffee mixture.

3. Gently spread with half the remaining sponge mixture and scatter with the remaining coffee mixture. Top with the remaining sponge mixture.

4. Toss the remaining tablespoon of sugar with the flaked almonds and cinnamon and scatter over the surface. Bake in a preheated oven, 180°C (350°F), Gas Mark 4, for 45 minutes until just firm and a skewer inserted into the centre comes out clean. Leave in the tin for 10 minutes, then transfer to a wire rack to cool. Drizzle with the coffee liqueur before serving.

White chocolate summer berry cake

This creamy cake is packed with white chocolate and berries.
The sponge can be made a day in advance and the cake
assembled a few hours before serving.

Preparation time 40 minutes, plus cooling
Cooking time 30 minutes
Serves 12

5 eggs
150 g (5 oz) caster sugar
150 g (5 oz) plain flour
75 g (3 oz) white chocolate, grated
50 g (2 oz) unsalted butter, melted
200 g (7 oz) strawberries
200 g (7 oz) raspberries
300 ml (½ pint) double cream
4 tablespoons orange liqueur
1 quantity White Chocolate Ganache (see page 59)

❶ Grease and line the bases of 2 sandwich tins, each
20 cm (8 inches) across. Grease the paper. Beat the
eggs and sugar in a heatproof bowl over a pan of hot
water until the whisk leaves a trail when lifted from
the bowl. Remove from the heat and whisk for a
further 2 minutes. Sift the flour over the mixture,
sprinkle with the chocolate and fold in. Drizzle the
melted butter over the mixture and fold in.

❷ Divide between the tins and bake in a preheated oven,
180°C (350°F), Gas Mark 4, for 25–30 minutes or until
just firm. Transfer to a wire rack to cool. Reserve a
handful of the fruits and lightly mash the remainder.
Whip the cream until just peaking. Halve each cake
and drizzle with the liqueur. Spread a layer with one-
third of the whipped cream and one-third of the fruits.

❸ Repeat the layering, finishing with a cake layer. Spread
a little ganache over the cake to seal in any crumbs.

❹ Swirl the remaining ganache over the sides of the
cake. Scatter with the reserved fruits.

Chocolate chip scones with citrus butter

These chocolate-studded scones are incredibly easy to make.
You needn't even wait for them to cool – they're delicious served
warm, split and buttered.

Preparation time 20 minutes
Cooking time 12 minutes
Makes 8 scones

225 g (7½ oz) self-raising flour
1 teaspoon baking powder
125 g (4 oz) unsalted butter
100 g (3½ oz) plain or milk chocolate, finely chopped
50 g (2 oz) icing sugar
about 150 ml (¼ pint) milk, plus extra to glaze
finely grated rind of ½ small orange, plus 2 teaspoons juice

❶ Grease a baking sheet. Sift the flour and baking
powder into a bowl. Add 40 g (1½ oz) butter, cut into
small pieces, and rub in with your fingertips until
the mixture resembles fine breadcrumbs. Stir in the
chocolate, 25 g (1 oz) icing sugar and 125 ml (4 fl oz)
milk and mix to a soft dough, adding the remaining
milk if the dough feels dry.

❷ Turn the dough on to a lightly floured surface and roll
out to 2 cm (¾ inch) thick. Use a 6 cm (2½ inch) cutter
to cut out rounds, re-rolling and cutting out the
trimmings as necessary.

❸ Transfer to the baking sheet and brush with milk to
glaze. Bake in a preheated oven, 220°C (425°F), Gas
Mark 7, for 12 minutes until well risen and pale golden.
Transfer to a wire rack to cool.

❹ Meanwhile, beat together the remaining butter and
sugar with the orange rind and juice and turn into
a small serving dish, ready for spreading over the
warm scones.

Crumbly raspberry and oat slices

Just like a dessert crumble, these little cakes provide that delicious contrast between crispy chunks of buttery crumble and bursts of tangy fruit.

Preparation time 15 minutes
Cooking time 1 hour
Makes 12–14 fingers

100 g (3½ oz) plain flour
75 g (3 oz) plain wholemeal flour
175 g (6 oz) porridge oats
175 g (6 oz) unsalted butter, slightly softened
150 g (5 oz) golden caster sugar
finely grated rind of 1 lemon
250 g (8 oz) fresh or frozen raspberries
icing sugar, for dusting

1 Lightly butter the base and sides of a shallow, 27 x 18 cm (10½ x 7 inch) rectangular baking tin or a similar sized roasting tin. Put the flours and oats in a bowl. Cut the butter into small pieces, add it to the dry ingredients and work with your fingers until the mixture makes a coarse crumble.

2 Stir in the sugar and lemon rind and continue to crumble the mixture together until it starts to cling together. Turn half the mixture into the tin and pat it down into an even layer.

3 Scatter the raspberries on top of the crumble mixture.

4 Sprinkle the remaining crumble mixture over the raspberries. Bake in a preheated oven, 180°C (350°F), Gas Mark 4, for about 1 hour or until the topping is turning golden. Cut into fingers and leave to cool in the tin. Serve dusted with icing sugar.

Strawberry shortcake

Laced with mascarpone-enriched cream and liqueur, this recipe makes a more extravagant strawberry shortcake than many versions. It's perfect for tea in the garden.

Preparation time 25 minutes

Cooking time about 35 minutes

Serves 8

175 g (6 oz) unsalted butter, softened

100 g (3½ oz) caster sugar

2 eggs, beaten

2 teaspoons vanilla extract

225 g (7½ oz) self-raising flour

1 teaspoon baking powder

250 g (8 oz) strawberries

100 g (3½ oz) raspberries

3 tablespoons Cointreau or other orange-flavoured liqueur

6 tablespoons redcurrant jelly

250 g (8 oz) mascarpone cheese

300 ml (½ pint) double cream

1 Lightly grease an 18 cm (7 inch) round cake tin. Cream together the butter and sugar until light and fluffy. Gradually beat in the eggs and vanilla extract. Sift the flour and baking powder into the bowl and stir until combined. Turn into the tin and level the surface. Bake in a preheated oven, 180°C (350°F), Gas Mark 4, for 30 minutes or until just firm to the touch. Transfer to a wire rack to cool.

2 Halve the strawberries and mix them in a bowl with the raspberries and 1 tablespoon liqueur. Cut the cake in half horizontally.

3 Melt the redcurrant jelly in a saucepan with 1 tablespoon water. Beat the mascarpone with the cream and remaining liqueur until peaking. Spread the base of the cake with half the mascarpone cream and scatter with half the fruits.

4 Brush with half the jelly and top with the remaining cake. Finish the top with the remaining cream, fruits and jelly and serve.

Kringle

This recipe is a simplified version of a traditional, sweet Danish bread: mildly spiced, fruity and baked in a pretzel shape. If liked, drizzle the surface of the cooled bread with glacé icing.

Preparation time 25 minutes, plus proving
Cooking time 30 minutes
Serves 10

2 teaspoons easy-blend dried yeast
75 g (3 oz) caster sugar, plus 1 teaspoon
200 ml (7 fl oz) hand-hot milk
400 g (13 oz) strong bread flour
crushed seeds of 15 cardamom pods
1 teaspoon ground mixed spice
1 egg, beaten, plus extra to glaze
75 g (3 oz) salted butter, melted
75 g (3 oz) sultanas
75 g (3 oz) blanched almonds, chopped
2 tablespoons icing sugar

① Stir the yeast and 1 teaspoon sugar into the milk in a small bowl and leave to stand for 10 minutes or until frothy. Mix the flour with the spices and remaining sugar. Add the egg, butter and yeasted milk and mix to a dough.

② Turn out on to a floured surface and knead gently for 10 minutes until smooth and elastic. Put in an oiled bowl, cover with clingfilm and leave to rise for about 1 hour or until doubled in size.

③ Knock back the dough (see page 53) and roll it out on a floured surface to a 45 x 15 cm (18 x 6 inch) rectangle.

④ Scatter with the sultanas and all but 15 g (½ oz) of the almonds and roll up.

⑤ Transfer to a greased baking sheet, curving into a knotted shape. Cover loosely with oiled clingfilm and leave to rise for 45 minutes or until doubled in size.

⑥ Brush the surface with beaten egg and dust with icing sugar. Scatter with the reserved nuts and bake in a preheated oven, 190°C (375°F), Gas Mark 5, for 30 minutes or until golden. Cool on a wire rack.

Thyme, orange and chocolate shortbread

Buttery homemade shortbread is always a real treat, and the subtle additions in this recipe make it even more irresistible.

Preparation time 15 minutes, plus chilling
Cooking time 20 minutes
Makes 25 pieces

1 tablespoon chopped thyme
50 g (2 oz) caster sugar
150 g (5 oz) milk or white chocolate, chopped
250 g (8 oz) plain flour
100 g (3½ oz) rice flour
finely grated rind of 1 orange
200 g (7 oz) lightly salted butter, diced

1 Grease 2 baking sheets. Reserve 1 teaspoon of the chopped thyme. Sprinkle the remainder over 25 g (1 oz) sugar on a chopping board and press the thyme into the sugar with the side of the knife. Melt the chocolate in a small bowl.

2 Sift the flour and rice flour into a mixing bowl. Add the reserved thyme, orange rind and butter and rub in with your fingertips until the mixture resembles coarse breadcrumbs.

3 Stir in the remaining sugar and the melted chocolate and mix with a round-bladed knife until the mixture starts to form a dough. Use your hands to bring the mixture together and turn it on to the work surface. Shape into a thick log, about 30 cm (12 inches) long. Roll it in greaseproof paper and chill for 1 hour.

4 Unwrap the log and roll it in the herb sugar.

5 Cut across into thick slices and space these slightly apart on the baking sheets. Bake in a preheated oven, 180°C (350°F), Gas Mark 4, for about 20 minutes until beginning to turn pale golden. Transfer to a wire rack to cool.

White chocolate biscotti

These gorgeous biscuits are baked in one piece, then sliced and re-baked to crisp them up. Serve the Italian way dunked into dessert wine or with some creamy hot chocolate.

Preparation time 15 minutes, plus cooling
Cooking time 35 minutes
Makes 24 biscuits

300 g (10 oz) white chocolate
25 g (1 oz) unsalted butter, softened
225 g (7½ oz) self-raising flour
50 g (2 oz) light muscovado sugar
2 eggs
1 teaspoon vanilla extract
100 g (3½ oz) pecan nuts, roughly chopped
icing sugar, for dusting

① Lightly grease a large baking sheet. Chop 100 g (3½ oz) chocolate into small pieces. Break up the remainder and melt it in a small bowl with the butter. Leave to cool. Sift the flour into a mixing bowl and stir in the sugar, eggs, vanilla extract, nuts and melted chocolate mixture.

② Add the chopped chocolate and mix to a dough. Tip the mixture on to a lightly floured surface and halve the dough.

③ Shape each half into a log about 25 cm (10 inches) long and flatten to a depth of 2 cm (¾ inch). Space well apart on the baking sheet and bake in a preheated oven, 190°C (375°F), Gas Mark 5, for 18–20 minutes until risen, golden and firm. Remove from the oven and reduce the oven temperature to 160°C (325°F), Gas Mark 3.

④ Leave the biscuit logs to cool for 20 minutes, then use a serrated knife to slice each length into slices 2 cm (¾ inch) thick. Space them slightly apart on the baking sheet and bake for a further 15 minutes. Dust with icing sugar and transfer to a wire rack to cool.

Chocolate cheesecake brownies

Instead of the classic sugary crust, these brownies are swirled with a delicious, marbly cheesecake topping.

Preparation time 20 minutes
Cooking time 30 minutes
Makes about 16 brownies

300 g (10 oz) plain chocolate, chopped
125 g (4 oz) lightly salted butter
150 g (5 oz) light muscovado sugar
75 g (3 oz) self-raising flour
75 g (3 oz) ground almonds
4 eggs
300 g (10 oz) mild soft goats' cheese
75 g (3 oz) caster sugar
1 teaspoon vanilla extract

1 Grease and line the base and sides of a shallow 28 x 20 cm (11 x 8 inch) baking tin. Grease the paper. Melt the chocolate with the butter in a medium-sized bowl.

2 Beat together the sugar, flour, ground almonds and 3 eggs in a mixing bowl to make a paste. Beat in the melted chocolate mixture.

3 In a separate bowl beat the cheese until softened. Beat in the sugar, remaining egg and the vanilla extract until smooth. Turn the chocolate mixture into the prepared tin, then spoon the cheese mixture on top.

4 Use a round-bladed knife to swirl the 2 mixtures gently together, lifting some of the chocolate mixture into the cheese topping, until lightly marbled. (Don't overwork the mixture or the flavours will completely merge together.)

5 Bake in a preheated oven, 190°C (375°F), Gas Mark 5, for about 30 minutes or until very softly set in the centre. Leave to cool in the tin, then serve cut into small rectangles.

Glacé fruits

Although the process is quite lengthy, it is worth the effort as homemade glacé fruits can be really delicious – use them in cakes, breads and sweets or to decorate desserts.

Preparation time 15 minutes
Cooking time over a period of 8 days

pineapple, sliced and then quartered
cherries, pitted but kept whole
firm pears, peeled, cored and halved
plums, stoned and halved
apricots, stoned and halved
granulated sugar

1 Cook all the fruit gently in sufficient water to cover until just tender. Drain and reserve the cooking liquid.

2 For each 500 g (1 lb) of fruit allow 300 ml (½ pint) of syrup. Make this by combining 300 ml (½ pint) of the water in which the fruits were cooked with 175 g (6 oz) sugar. Stir over a low heat until the sugar has fully dissolved.

3 Put the cooked fruit in a single layer in a shallow, non-metallic dish and pour over the warm syrup. Cover the dish and leave for 24 hours.

4 On day 2 drain the syrup from the fruit and measure it into a pan. Add 50 g (2 oz) sugar for each 300 ml (½ pint) syrup and bring to the boil. Pour over the fruit, cover and leave for 24 hours. Repeat this process 3 times more, each time adding an additional 50 g (2 oz) sugar to the syrup.

5 On day 6 drain the fruit, return the syrup to the pan and add 75 g (3 oz) sugar for each 300 ml (½ pint) of syrup. Bring to the boil, add the fruit and boil for 3 minutes. Return to the dish and leave for 24 hours.

6 Repeat step 5. The syrup should be like thick honey. If it is thin, repeat once again. Drain the syrup and arrange the fruit in a single layer on a wire rack set over a baking sheet. Leave to dry, then store in an airtight box between layers of waxed paper.

Pumpkin cake with vanilla caramel

Make the most of the relatively short pumpkin season with this autumnal cake. For the rest of the year orange-fleshed squash makes a good substitute.

Preparation time 30 minutes

Cooking time about 55 minutes

Serves 10

250 g (8 oz) pumpkin (skinned and deseeded weight)
175 g (6 oz) unsalted butter, softened
175 g (6 oz) light muscovado sugar
175 g (6 oz) self-raising flour
1 teaspoon baking powder
2 teaspoons ground coriander
3 eggs
75 g (3 oz) ground almonds

Vanilla caramel
100 g (3½ oz) caster sugar
2 tablespoons single cream
2 teaspoons vanilla extract

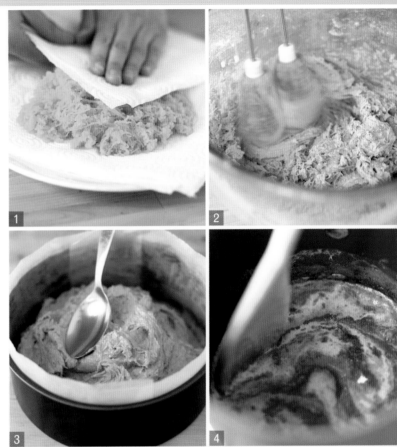

1 Grease and line the base and sides of a 20 cm (8 inch) round cake tin. Grease the paper. Finely grate the pumpkin and pat it dry on kitchen paper.

2 Put the butter, sugar, flour, baking powder, coriander, eggs and almonds in a bowl and beat until smooth and creamy.

3 Stir in the pumpkin, turn the mixture into the tin and level the surface. Bake in a preheated oven, 160°C (325°F), Gas Mark 3, for about 45 minutes or until a skewer inserted into the centre comes out clean. Transfer to a wire rack to cool.

4 Make the vanilla caramel. Put the sugar and 4 tablespoons water in a small, heavy-based saucepan and heat gently, stirring, until the sugar dissolves. Bring to the boil and boil until the syrup turns to a golden caramel. Remove from the heat and stir in the cream and vanilla extract. Heat gently until smooth. Transfer the cake to a serving plate and spoon over the caramel. Serve with extra caramel, if liked.

Index

Acknowledgements

Acknowledgements

Executive Editor: Jane Donovan
Editor: Charlotte Macey
Executive Art Editor: Karen Sawyer
Designer: One 2 Six Creative Ltd
Photographer: Stephen Conroy
Props Stylist: Rachel Jukes
Food Stylist: Joanna Farrow
Production Manager: Ian Paton
Picture Researcher: Taura Riley